introducing thousands to the Jesuit-Franciscan legacy from 1687 to 1832. The three-day, two-night pilgrimages before and after Easter and the *Día de los Muertos* focus on small villages and remote towns far from the main byways of tourists speeding to beaches. Bunny and other "talkers" would recall stories of colonial days and early independent Mexico between string *corridas* and other traditional songs from notable Ronstadts, Big Jim Griffith, and others fluent with trans-border music.

• Compiler of key evidence documenting traditional O'odham domains, their seizure over the years, and the looting of their water rights. That led to federal lawsuits and then to U.S. legislation signed by President Reagan in 1982 to restore those rights. The flatlands around San Xavier are again green with crops, and nearby the Santa Cruz flowed continually for over 18 months before the drought of 2020 and Covid-19 shutdowns of copper mines.

• Primary provider of materials for the San Xavier District's Tohono O'odham Library in its new administrative headquarters.

Bunny earned his Ph.D. in anthropology at the University of Arizona, and then served as an ethnologist at the Arizona State Museum, lecturer in the Dept. of Anthropology, and field historian for the UA Library. From 1956 the Fontanas lived less than a mile west of San Xavier. Hazel Fontana, "the better half of the team," contributed the art for this history and designed the fountain in the mission's courtyard. An honors art graduate at Berkeley, her work appeared in *Arizona & the West* and *Journal of the Southwest*, in *Smoke Signal* No. 5 "Alamos – Sonora's City of Silver", and in Edward Spicer's *Cycles of Conquest* (Tucson: University of Arizona Press, 1962).

Other Contributors

Edward McCain is the digital curator at the Reynolds Journalism Institute at the University of Missouri at Columbia. He has lectured on photography at universities and workshops nationwide, and in 2003 won the *Arizona Highways* Gold Award for Photographic Excellence. His work has appeared in *Sunset*, *Sports Illustrated*, *U.S. News & World Report*, and many other publications. Over 190 of his color photographs appear in *A Gift of Angels: The Art of Mission San Xavier del Bac.*

Editor and 2016-2021 updater David Carter is a docent with the Patronato San Xavier. He was its secretary from 2007 to 2016 and continues on the Conservation Committee. At SMRC he is a director and leader on its Kino Mission Tours. At the University of Arizona he designed the 1.3-acre U.S.S. *Arizona* Mall Memorial dedicated in 2016. From 1983 to 2020 he was a designer-builder in the Barrio Libre and in 2006 designed the new sanctuary at St. Ambrose Church. From 1978 to 1986 he was a reporter, editor, and columnist at the Arizona Daily Star. He earned an M.A. in philosophy, politics, & economics at Hertford College, Oxford on a Rhodes scholarship after a B.A. in government & journalism at Arizona.

✦ ✦ ✦ ✦ ✦

DEI

To all my friends and neig...
Thank you for all you have given me.
    – Bernard "Bunny" Fontana, 2015

CONTENTS

A compact, year-round Sobaipuri village of rows of paired dirt-topped houses and storage quarters along the Santa Cruz and San Pedro rivers (Scott Seibel).

1691: an epochal year for Bac or Vaak or, as now known, Wa:k —

the site where water washing over sand and rocks goes in or enters in subterranean passages: the sudden end of over two miles of almost continual and thus life-nurturing and life-enriching surface flows (Winters 2020: 762).

Before submerging at Bac into the underlying aquifer, what today we call the Santa Cruz River meandered north to Bac year-round across a broad flood plain. Its shallow but usually reliable downstream flows allowed for gravity and simple ditches to channel water east, west, and north to slightly lower but nearby fields. The resulting harvests supported some 800 Sobaipuri O'odham and the largest village of the vast Pimería Alta in what is now Southern Arizona and Northern Sonora (Webb et al. 2014: 37, 43-44; Kino 1948: I:122; Polzer 1998: 43).

Despite its relative wealth, Bac decided by 1691 to invite and embrace radical change. For two to three years the villagers had likely scouted and asked about an impressive newcomer some 110 miles to the south – a European in black robes introducing new crops, livestock, and tools as well as a new creed. First at Dolores southeast of Magdalena and then at nearby villages, fields were enlarged and herds expanded (Burrus 1971: 38-41). The Sobaipuri had seen the Coronado expedition in 1540 and 1542 and Spanish

expansion into central Sonora over the last 50 years, but now it had come even closer (Fontana 1994: 26-28; Roca 124-205).

Talks about these changes probably went on for months. But in the first week of 1691 word spread that Padre Francisco Eusebio Kino and another black robe of the Society of Jesus were almost half way to the village. The headmen apparently agreed: find Kino and urge him to come to Bac (Kessell 1966: 57-63).

Kino's memoirs recall escorting his greatest Jesuit contemporary Fr. Visitor Juan María Salvatierra, for circa 50 miles northwest over 11 days to Tubutama on Epiphany, January 6th. They met "more than 500 souls," then rode north another 25 miles to Tucubavia, about 10 miles west of modern Nogales, counting "more than 700 souls, who received us everywhere with great pleasure."

After baptizing infants and accepting gifts, "it was our intention to turn back," Kino writes ...

> *but from the north some messengers or couriers of the Sobaipuris of San Xavier del Bac...and from San Cayetano del Tumagacori came to meet us with some crosses which they gave us, kneeling with great veneration, and asking us on behalf of all their people to go to their rancherías also.*

The padres rode to Tumacácori, and there they met Sobaipuri headmen instead of couriers from Bac. They found "three arbors one in which to say Mass, another in which to sleep, and the third for a kitchen." More infants were baptized but then the Jesuits, with promises that padres would be coming, had to return south (Kino 1948: I: 24,119-120).

Bac had taken the first big step, but would have to wait till late August or early September 1692 for Kino's first visit.

A long evolving legacy

Limited evidence suggests that small groups may have ranged around the Tucson Basin as early as 11,500 B.C. (Doelle 2018a). In the San Pedro valley to the southeast near today's border they hunt mammoth, great bison, and an ancient horse, all now extinct. Rainfall of about 40 inches a year supports rich grasslands with rivers and bogs lined by oak and hickory. About 10,000 B.C. the last Ice Age ends. Glaciers melt and recede from what become the Great Lakes. Sea levels rise, shrinking Baja California and widening the Gulf of California. Far to the north the new Bering Strait separates Alaska from Siberia, severing the Western Hemisphere from the Old World. The New World is cut off, but continues to evolve. An approximate timeline:

• **7500 B.C.** Temperatures warm, rainfall drops, and large trees die off at lower elevations. Game is smaller – mule deer, pronghorn antelope, pig-like peccary, and jaguar. Foraging turns seasonal over smaller areas. Grinding stones help convert seeds to food.

• **2100 B.C.** Farming begins along the Santa Cruz floodplain, including plantings of a now extinct maize domesticated far south into Mexico – a small-cobbed popcorn. The yield is still too meager to substantially replace a diet of over 30 seasonal wild plants, but tending to the plants and its restraint of forays far away leads to the earliest known structures in the Tucson Basin: pit houses built just west of downtown. These are small round dwellings of saplings, brush, and reeds with floors about a step below the outside terrain – a shallow pit. And here is some of the most extensive evidence of continuous habitation in the United States (Diehl 2018: 16; Doelle 2018a: 3; Thiel 2018a: 11).

• **1500 to 1200 B.C.** Irrigation arises to water more fields, then within 300 years engineering creates sophisticated, extensive, and likely cooperatively owned and managed canals, but with fields and harvests belonging to individual households. Farmers can adjust to droughts and even catastrophic floods.

• **A.D. 50** Beans and squash are recent arrivals in the Tucson Basin, joining a much-advanced maize as dietary staples. Instead of baskets or animal hide bags stored underground, true pottery is produced in quantity for the first time in today's Southwest. Seeds and other foods can be stored safely and for far longer in large sealed pots. People begin building more permanent pit houses: either oval or square, or rectangular with rounded corners. Larger structures may be for ritual and community gatherings. Larger harvests lead to larger populations. People acquire shell, turquoise, obsidian, and other goods from far away (J. Vint 2018: 15; Diehl 2018: 16-17; Thiel 2018b: 17).

A 5-gallon seed jar circa A.D. 450, Tucson Basin (Desert Archaeology Inc.).

• **A.D. 500** Clusters of Hohokam households become true villages of cooperating families along the Santa Cruz and begin to produce for trade decorated red-on-brown wares with bold geometric designs or stylized human and animal figures. Pit houses often cluster around courtyards with their entries facing the common area. Canals are greatly expanded.

• **750:** Large centralized villages arise near rivers, along with smaller settlements and outlying seasonal camps to support hunting, gathering, or limited farming (Doelle & Thiel 2018: 21-22).

• **800 to 1000:** Villages in the Tucson Basin build at least 24 large ballcourts including four within today's San Xavier District. Traces of six more ballcourt villages are suspected below modern buildings and streets. Quantities of dirt are moved to create the sunken courts framed by raised berms where different communities meet, mingle, and exchange goods and foods (Doelle & Thiel 2018: 22; Doelle 2018b: 24). Near Martínez Hill east of San Xavier and Interstate 19, one of the ballcourts is 150 feet north to south and 60 feet across.

Visualization of a ballcourt akin to those near Martínez Hill east of San Xavier. At right, large pit houses in front, smaller ones possibly for storage to the rear (Robert B. Ciaccio, Desert Archaeology Inc.).

- **1000:** Foraging for wild foods declines. Canals by 1000 allow for irrigated crops producing predictably bountiful harvests. Clusters of courtyards include a roasting area and a cemetery for cremains. Oversized square houses are built bordering plazas, possibly for clan leaders. Others live in small houses behind the big ones and away from the plaza. Over the generations, selective planting of the best seeds creates large-cobbed high-yield maize we would recognize today (Diehl 2018: 17; Wallace 2018: 25).

- **1150:** Ballcourts are abandoned. Hohokam villagers begin building above-ground earthen compounds that supplement but never wholly replace the simpler pit houses. Some walls are reinforced with rows of vertical posts and others with cobbles, but all are built with a stiff clay-sand-dirt mix slathered in place to harden level by level. Agave is farmed for food and fiber.

High Hohokam at Martínez Hill

Excavations near Martínez Hill in 1929-1931 found what is now recognized as up to 4 or more platform mounds, and 5 more mounds (not all necessarily platform mounds) were found nearby in 1995. Both sites apparently have extensive adobe room blocks consisting of long rows of adjacent adobe rooms including double rows (Wallace & Holmlund 1984: 181-183).

At the first complex stones weighing 50 to 75 pounds or more were found top to bottom in mud fill up to 7 feet high in 20 of the rooms. The largest platform mound is 70 feet north to south and 64 feet across. Walls and apparent room blocks over 400 feet long run to another mound 80 feet north to south and 44 feet across.

Exterior walls were rough and irregular, but on interior walls a very fine caliche plaster provided a hard and smooth finish. In at least some areas the plaster was applied by hand. Doorways were few. Entry to most rooms before they were filled was from above. Floors of smooth caliche are often 4 or 5 inches thick and almost as hard as concrete (Gabel 1931: 1-37; Wallace & Holmlund 1984: 181-183).

Conjectural view of circa 1300 platform mounds and earthen-walled compounds east of San Xavier and I-19 near Martínez Hill (Doug Gann, Chronos Digital LLC).

About the same time, massive volcanic rock walls called *trincheras*, cultivated narrow terraces, pit houses, and possibly ritual sites are built on the middle and upper slopes of Martínez Hill, at Black Mountain to the southwest, and at Tumamoc Hill to the north. These are smaller versions of *trincheras* architecture from perhaps 800 in today's Sonora south of the Hohokam periphery. Long loose-laid contours of rock walls predominate on northeast to northwest slopes. Small harvests from winter rains are possible because of fewer freezes, higher minimum temperatures, and moisture-retaining volcanic clay soils. Lookouts are perhaps a bonus but by 1300 these outposts are abandoned (Downum et al. 2009).

- **1275 to 1300:** Most of the smaller villages across the Tucson Basin are abandoned, but in at least six of the largest villages the Hohokam begin to build big dirt-walled compounds with two to three or more platform mounds. These multistory structures are built throughout Southern Arizona and especially in Central Arizona, notably at the Casa Grande. They are thick-walled rectangles deliberately filled with dirt and rocks to create a platform or raised terrace 5- to 6-feet high or even higher behind a low parapet. Sometimes habitable rooms are built atop part of the terrace while some of the rooms may be primarily ceremonial structures. Either way this is architecture requiring organized and likely directed labor, perhaps evidence of differences in power and social rank within the community (Doelle et al. 2018: 28-29).

- **1300 to 1400:** In the late 1200s a long drought in what is now northeastern Arizona leads thousands to migrate south below the Mogollon Rim. Some move eventually into the San Pedro valley near Redington Pass. Most settle amicably among the eastern fringe of the Hohokam despite different traditions. They are a minority, but into the late 1300s nurture what archaeologists call the Salado culture, keen on cooperation and trade. Their distinctive pots of red, black, and white are exchanged across much of Hohokam domains, including the Zanardelli village about 6 miles south of Bac (Clark 2020: 1-11; Doelle et al. 2018: 29; Jones et al. 2018: 29).

- **1400 to 1450:** Almost all the large settlements of the Gila Watershed are depopulated from 1400 to 1450. The Salado as well as the Hohokam become archaeologically invisible. The Sobaipuris in the Tucson Basin are living very differently in terms of the material traces they leave behind, but persist and prevail.

- **1450 to 1691:** To many, the Tucson Basin is part of the traditional territory of the Sobaipuri and other O'odham since time immemorial, yet their stories talk about a different path (Doelle 2018a: 3; Seymour 2011: 11). Archaeologist Deni Seymour, a longtime specialist on the Sobaipuri, says that

> In the 1400s (and likely earlier), after the reorganization and decimation of prehistoric populations noted in O'odham traditional stories, some Sobaipuri sites show hints that perhaps remnant Hohokam, Salado, or Trincheras populations were co-residing with the Sobaipuri. This of course implies that the Sobaipuri were newcomers and that they incorporated these people into their own. This is consistent with some traditional accounts that have the O'odham migrating in, taking out the local leaders with their magic, and leveling buildings in battle. Other accounts indicate that after the wars the compliant commoners were allowed to stay, ultimately becoming O'odham....[The] stories vary about this period because it was so long ago and because different groups residing in different areas probably experienced this transition in different ways (Seymour 2011: 11-12).

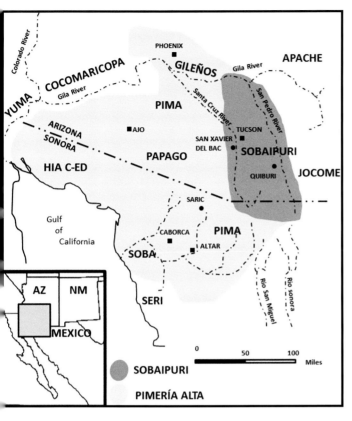

Circa 1690: Sobaipuri domain within the Pimería Alta (Deni Seymour).

Mastering arid terrain

Either way, water allowed the Sobaipuri in the Santa Cruz and San Pedro valleys to grow as much as 40 percent of their food in floodplain fields of corn, beans, and squash. That was about twice the harvest of their cousins to the west, the Tohono or desert O'odham who depended on direct summer rains and brush weirs or shallow berms in arroyos to trap water for low-land crops.

Sobaipuri domains received more rain than land to the west, about 10 to 15 inches annually depending on elevation versus 5 to 10 inches for Tohono lands. With their richer oasis habitat the Sobapuris grew cotton as well as tobacco. They relied less on hunting and on the seasonal gathering of wild plants and insects. They could live in year-round villages. They didn't need to continually migrate between summer fields and higher winter camps near springs or shallow wells in the foothills or mountains.

The fruit of cacti as well as mesquite pods and various greens helped supplement the harvests. Edible insects included locusts, cicadas, larvae, and worms. Hunters brought in the meat, hides, horns, and many other usable parts of deer, pronghorn antelope, bighorn sheep, bobcats, kit foxes, rabbits, tortoises, and all sorts of lizards plus ducks, doves, and quail. Grass, reeds, brush, branches, and saguaro ribs could be gathered nearby for houses, storage enclosures, sunshade ramadas, and fires for cooking and for creating pots (Fontana 1976: 62-68; 1996b: 19, 21-23).

Women wove baskets (at times water-tight) from willow, devil's claw, and reeds, and in makeshift kilns fired clay pots for water and cooking. Seeds were ground to flour with a hand-held stone *mano*

over a large, flat *metate*. Small rock arrowheads on shafts shot from carved willow bows could create only minor wounds, but poison made them lethal (Fontana 1976: 49, 56, 58-60).

Men met in nightly council talks in a brush structure called the rain house *(vahki)*, round house *(olas ki)*, or big house *(gu ki)*. Amidst ceremonial regalia they decided matters by consensus, agreeing on plans for rites such as the all-important saguaro wine feast for bringing rain. The ceremonies themselves would be outside on cleared ground east of the entry to the meeting house. In the mornings, the town crier would climb onto its roof or above the adjoining ramada to shout out instructions for the day: a rabbit hunt, clearing fields, gathering wood, or whatever the community chores might be. Family dwellings had to be within earshot.

Village headmen held office by dint of their abilities rather than through inheritance. Wise Speaker was the ritual orator. Keeper of the Smoke was the organizer and principal speaker at council talks. Keeper of the Plaited Basket guarded the council's sacred bundle. And The One Above was a great man. The headman was more moderator and conciliator than authoritarian figure or autocrat – never an overall leader except in times of war or threat of war (Fontana 1996b: 25-26; Sheridan 1988: 156).

The trajectories of the sun, moon, and stars guided travelers and marked the seasons: times to plant and when to harvest.

Into the early 1900s, O'odham economies were based on generosity and sharing. Ceremonial exchanges, gifts, and betting on inter-village games disbursed available resources. Stinginess was a cardinal vice. The O'odham lived amidst scarcity, but behaved as if surrounded by abundance. People invested in family, friends, and neighbors rather than material wealth. Cooperation was the key to desert survival. Men and women shared much of the work. One's family and community bonds were always paid-up insurance.

O'odham *hímdag* is the whole way of daily life and activities, a living ethic. Various mammals, amphibians, reptiles, birds, and insects as well as lightning, wind, the sea, enemies, and "women of the darkness" (harlots) possess *hímdag* and potentially dangerous *géwkadag* (strength). *Hímdag* did much to moderate daily behavior and explain a whole class of illnesses.

Important public ceremonies focused on crops, hunting, warfare, community well-being, and, most important of all, "bringing down the clouds." In the desert, rain meant life, so a great deal of devotion was directed toward invoking that blessing.

Language was perhaps the highest O'odham art. Speeches, ritual oratory, and song lyrics are powerful and poetic. The grammar is as subtle and complex as any in the world; its vocabulary is rich in words defining the external and internal (Fontana 1996b: 26-27).

Till at least the 1920s, gourd rattles *(cakot)* were used with songs to bring rain and care for the sick. Three other instruments were scraping sticks *(hiohkat)*, drums made of inverted baskets *(tamoa)*, and reed flutes (Densmore 1929: 3-4). Music begat dancing with or without lyrics, and whether traditional songs or new sounds from Europe. Jesuits Joseph Och and Ignaz Pfefferkorn arrived in Sonora in 1756, with Och recalling years later that, thanks to string instrumentals, his colleague attracted followers early on at today's Atil some 90 miles south-southwest of Bac –

Sivariano Garcia with hand-made cane flute at San Xavier early 1920 (Smithsonian Institution).

Fr. Pfefferkorn (who would not have been out of place in a company of violin virtuosos) accomplished with music what he could not with exhortation ... his audience of Indians in the village of Atí gathered around so that when he looked through his window he could see old and young dancing. Little by little all the houses surrounded his, for some of the sturdy inhabitants pulled up their house walls and pushed them, thatch-roof and all, nearer to his dwelling (Och 1965: 152).

In most of the pre-Columbian Western Hemisphere cut off for over 12,000 years from the mingling of new discoveries in Africa, Asia, and Europe, the O'odham, Hohokam, and earlier cultures evolved political, social, and economic traditions admirably attuned to survival in deserts high and low. Their existence, however, was far from utopian. Food supplies were often precarious. There were surely times of starvation. Life expectancy was probably short. The only domesticated animals were dogs. And although most men and some women were notable long-distance runners, travel was limited to what they could traverse afoot, and thus with minimal baggage (Fontana 1996b: 26-27; Sheridan 1996: 56; Underhill 1936: 7-9, 29-32).

The Sobaipuris in 1691 were well aware that Kino and the Spanish might be valuable military allies versus other Indians, especially the Western Apaches. Historian Tom Sheridan says that the O'odham (Pimans) may also have seen Kino and other missionaries as a powerful new type of *mákai* or shaman able to communicate with supernaturals and exercise powers not known in the universe of the O'odham. He concludes:

Whatever the exact nature of Piman perceptions at contact, we do know this: if the Northern Pimans had become enemies rather than allies of the Spaniards, there would be no Tucson, no Tubac, and certainly no Mission San Xavier. Without the help of the Pimans, the Spaniards could never have held their northwestern frontier (Sheridan 1988: 153).

Prelude to Kino

Over 150 years before Padre Kino, Alvar Núñez Cabeza de Vaca, two other Spaniards, and a Moroccan slave, Esteban, came close to entering what is now Arizona in April 1536. On foot, they stumbled onto fellow Spaniards in Sonora, thus ending an eight-year voyage and overland trek from Florida across much of the Southwest. Cabeza de Vaca spread rumors of cities of gold lying to the north, and Nueva España began to explore beyond its northern frontier. Esteban led a Franciscan friar, Marcos de Niza, into today's Arizona in late April or early May 1539 and then into New Mexico. Fray Marcos returned with his own tales of cities of gold – the fabled Seven Cities of Cíbola.

In late June 1540, the good friar, who was later accused of not allowing facts to interfere with a fine story, accompanied Francisco Vásquez de Coronado and an expedition of over 400 Europeans, more than 1,000 Indians, and a long mobile food train of cattle, sheep, and goats. Coronado descended the San Pedro River into Arizona within some 65 miles from Bac before turning northeast at Lewis Springs toward New Mexico and eventually as far as Kansas. Two years later a depleted expedition retreated along the same route, having found no cities of gold (Brasher 2007: 437-460). To supply Coronado and his men, Hernando de Alarcón sailed up the lower Colorado River between Arizona and California. Melchior Díaz, soldier and mayor of Culiacán, Sinaloa, may have entered Arizona near Lukeville. He trekked west and northwest to the Colorado looking for Alarcón, but never found him.

Over 60 years later in 1604-05, Don Juan de Oñate led a party of about 35 men from New Mexico across Northern Arizona down the Colorado to within sight of its mouth and back again. Nonetheless, in Southern Arizona, the northern frontier of Nueva España in 1540-42 and 1604-05 remained just that – a frontier – and so it was after another 80 years when Kino arrived to rescue men's souls (Fontana 1994: 19-22, 25-29, 63).

Founder of Mission San Xavier: Fr. Francisco Eusebio Kino as shown in the 1965 statue by Suzanne Silvercruys in the U.S. Capitol (Architect of the Capitol).

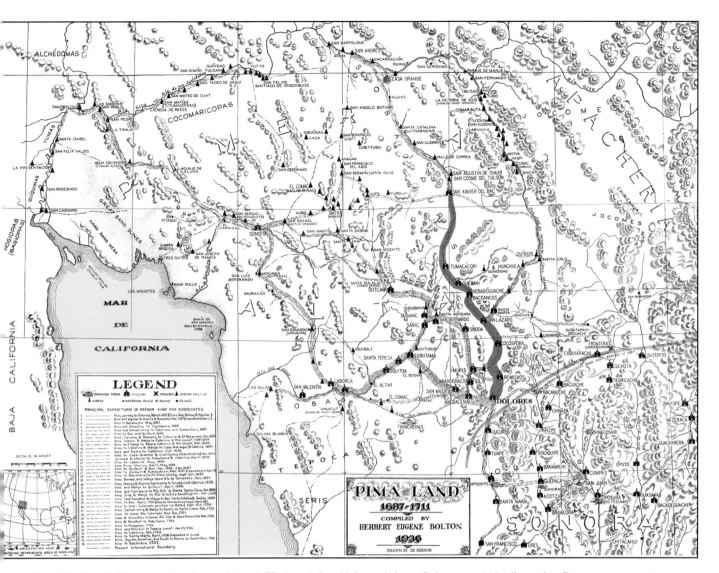

The 1687 Rim of Christendom in yellow and, in red, Kino's path from his base mission at Dolores some 110 miles north to Bac (H.E. Bolton: UA Press).

Padre Kino founds
Mission San Xavier: 1692-1702

Dust eddied over the stream. Summer rains had ended and the trail beside the Santa María – today's Santa Cruz River – was already dry. Days were hot but evenings brought a hint of oncoming fall as Father Kino, some Indian officials, his servants, and 50 pack animals trekked north to the "principal ranchería of San Xavier del Bac, which contains more than 800 souls," and where they found, "the natives very affable and friendly" (Kino 1948: 1: 122).

On his first visit to Bac, Kino:

> *...spoke to them of the Word of God, and on a map of the world showed them the lands, the rivers, and the seas over which we fathers had come from afar to bring them the saving knowledge of our holy faith. And I told them also how in ancient times the Spaniards were not*

Christians, how Santiago came to teach them the faith, and how for the first 14 years he was able to baptize only a few, because of which the holy apostle was discouraged, but that the most holy Virgin appeared to him and consoled him, telling him that Spaniards would convert the rest of the people of the world. And I showed them on the map of the world how the Spaniards and the faith come by sea to Vera Cruz, and had gone in to Puebla and to México, Guadalaxara, Sinaloa, and Sonora, and now to Nuestra Señora de los Dolores del Cósari, in the land of the Pimas [O'odham], where there were already many persons baptized, a house, church, bells, and images of saints, plentiful supplies, wheat, maize, and many cattle and horses; that they could go and see it all, and even ask at once of their relatives, my servants, who were with me. They listened with pleasure to these and other talks concerning God, heaven, and hell, and told me that they wished to be Christians, and gave me some infants to baptize. These Sobaipuris are in a very fine valley of the Río de Santa María (Kino 1948: 1: 122-23).

In May 1694, Lt. Antonio de Solís of the Compañía Volante, a troop of Spanish cavalry, passed through San Xavier in search of stolen horses, killing innocent and peaceful Indians along the way (Manje 1954: 7, 47). Six months later, in November, Kino set out to find the ruins of Casa Grande. Capt. Juan Mateo Manje, who

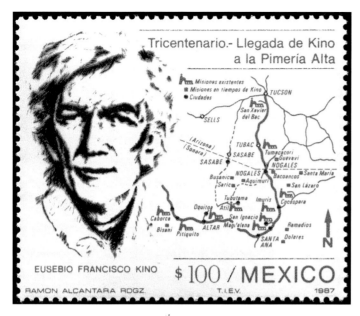

1987 Mexican stamp marks 300th anniversary of Kino's arrival in Sonora.

accompanied Kino on nine major trips from 1694 to 1701, had heard reports about the abandoned three-story structure built of rammed earth. Kino had given the tale little credence until he heard the same story from Indians from San Xavier who visited him at his home mission at Dolores. En route to becoming the first European to see the now-famous Casa Grande south of the Gila River, Kino apparently again passed through San Xavier (Kino 1948: I: 127 n. 128).

While enhancing Spanish knowledge of the Pimería Alta, Kino broadened native culture in introducing livestock, grains, garbanzos, lentils, cabbage, onions, garlic, leeks, cowpeas, sugarcane, mustard, mint, anise, pepper, new melons, grapes, apples, peaches, quince, plums, pomegranates, apricots, and figs. The most important new food was winter wheat. Instead of perhaps two plantings grown from March through October, fields could be farmed year-round. Hard frosts were no longer devastating, and with the help of new tools from the Old World, the O'odham could produce possibly twice as much food (Sheridan 1988: 157).

On Jan. 13, 1697 on his third trip to Bac, the Jesuit frontiersman delivered cattle, sheep, goats, and a small drove of mares:

I was received with all love by the many inhabitants of the great rancheria, and by many other principal men, who had gathered from various parts adjacent. The word of God was spoken to them, there were baptisms of little ones, and beginnings of good sowings and harvests of wheat for the father minister whom they asked for and hoped to receive (Kino 1948: I: 165).

The Sobaipuris at Bac anticipated the arrival of a resident priest. On Kino's return to the village in November 1697, he and Manje were given lodging in "the adobe house constructed with beams and a flat roof" which the natives "had built ... for the missionary priest they had been offered" (Manje 1954: 93). Kino's influence was taking effect. His party was greeted by Sobaipuris who placed woven arches and crosses in front of them, swept the roads in their path, and supplied cattle, sheep, goats, and even fresh bread baked in the new oven Kino had ordered at Bac (Kino 1948: I: 173-174; Manje 1954: 93).

On Sept. 26, 1698 Kino arrived in Bac about 4 in the afternoon with Capt. Diego Carrasco to meet up with 40 pack animals sent ahead five days earlier. The next afternoon they set out via San Cosme del Tucsón for San Agustín Oyaur [Oiaur], 13 miles to the north on their way to the Gila River and then the Pinacates (Kino 1966: 13-14).

On the padre's sixth visit on March 7, 1699, Capt. Manje recorded that 1,300 villagers

were congregated to celebrate our arrival with dancing and songs. As it was the rainy season, we were compelled to delay our journey and remained there for two days. In accordance with their custom, they made us presents and showed us 100 fanegas of wheat [about 7¼ cubic yards], which they had harvested and stored in the adobe and flat roofed house. They also showed us many cattle and mares, which they were taking care of until they are given a priest. From this neighborhood alone, with its rich lands all under irrigation, a mission of 3,000 souls could be established. During the two days that we remained here we were kept busy explaining to them the mysteries of our Holy Faith (Manje 1954: 125).

The Sobaipuri wish to have their own missionary and a church at Bac came a step closer on Kino's next visit on Oct. 29, 1699. Accompanied by the Rev. Fr. Visitor Antonio Leal, by a fellow Pimería Jesuit, Fr. Francisco Gonzalvo, and by Manje, Kino recorded the visit in his field diary as shown at right (Kino 1991: [22]).

The next day the governor of the Pápagos living in the desert west of Bac, apparently from the village of Anegam near today's Sells, arrived with ten other Indians to greet the Father Visitor and Kino. That evening Manje and Fr. Leal climbed a nearby hill, probably that now known as Grotto Hill east of today's mission, and pulled a white, loaf-shaped rock from its top. A great wind storm arose, lasting all night and until early morning when the Indians climbed the hill and replaced the rock, which they called the door to the House of the Wind. On, Nov. 1, Kino and Manje left on an inspection trip to the Gila River while Leal and Gonzalvo remained at Bac. Before Kino's return on Nov. 4, Fr. Leal counted more than 3,000 Indians in the immediate vicinity of San Xavier. He was convinced that the fertile irrigated land, not to mention the fine grazing land for cattle and horses, would support a mission of at least 3,000 inhabitants. He promised the Sobaipuris, whose kindness pleased him, that they would have Fr. Gonzalvo as their resident priest as soon as it could be arranged (Kino 1948: I: 205-07; Manje 1954: 136-141).

April 26 to May 2, 1700 was a momentous week at San Xavier. Kino arrived on the 26th on his eighth trip to the village and promptly sent word by messenger that the Indian leaders in the region should assemble at Bac. He was anxious to question them about the blue abalone shells he had seen inland in the Pimería Alta. These blue shells, it proved, came only from the Pacific, not from the Gulf of California, and were traded overland by Indians from the California coast. This was the proof Kino sought to show that California was not an island, but part of the mainland, and that an overland route to California was indeed feasible (Ives 1961; Martin 1954: 39-42).

San Xavier was thriving. Kino said his party killed:

... six beeves of the 300 which they were tending for me here, with 40 head of sheep and goats, and a small drove of mares. They also had a good field of wheat which was beginning to head; and during the following days they planted for the church a large field of maize, which they had previously cleared (Kino 1948: I: 235).

[On April 28:] *... we began the foundations of a very large and capacious church and house of San Xavier del Bac, all the many people working with much pleasure and zeal, some in digging the foundations, others in hauling many very good stones of tezontle from a little hill*

29 OCTOBER 1699:
KINO'S FIELD DIARY FROM SAN XAVIER

On the 29th at about two in the afternoon and after traveling 10 leagues, we arrived at San Xavier del Bac in the land of the western Sobaipuris. More than 40 children, all with crosses in their hands, came out to receive us. The road was cleaned and lined with crosses and arches. Then, bearing foods of many kinds, more than 300 adults arrived. Later we counted over a thousand souls for soon others came in from farther away. In anticipation of the arrival of a (resident) Father there was an earthen-roofed adobe house, and they had cattle and sheep, more than 30 head of each, a harvest of maize, a good planting of wheat already sprouting, and the 66 remounts (for the expedition). We butchered two fat steers and a sheep. Pastures and planting fields are so extensive, with so many earthen aqueducts filled with plentiful water, that the Father Visitor remarked that an outlay such as theirs in this glorious valley could provision another city as large as Mexico City (Kino 1991).

which was about a quarter of a league away. For the mortar for these foundations it was not necessary to haul water, because by means of the irrigation ditches we very easily conducted the water where we wished. And that house, with its great court and garden nearby, will be able to have throughout the year all the water it may need, running to any place or work room one may please, and one of the greatest and best fields in all Nueva Biscaya (Kino 1948: 1: 235-236).

Work continued on the foundations the next day, and Indian officials continued to arrive at Bac. Kino asked them about the blue shells, but on May 2 returned to his mission of Dolores. With him was the son of the principal captain of Bac to learn prayers, Christian doctrine, and how to assist at Mass (Kino 1948: 1: 236-239).

While still at San Xavier on this visit, Kino had written Fr. Visitor Leal saying he wished to be replaced at Dolores so that he might become Bac's first resident priest. Leal agreed in principle, so Kino promptly sent 700 of the 1,400 head of cattle at Dolores to San Xavier and the Sobaipuris built new corrals. But there was no replacement for Kino at Dolores, and he was in demand to find the overland route to California (Kino 1948: I: 240-241).

The day after leaving Bac, Kino was about to prove again that he was a superb equestrian. At Tumacácori at sunrise he was preparing to celebrate Mass when a messenger arrived with a letter. Fr. Agustín de Campos in San Ignacio asked Kino to help save a poor prisoner who the local soldiers had decided to execute the next day. After the Mass, Kino rode south and mostly uphill for over 70 miles, arriving almost at midnight at Ímuris. He reports that "the next day very early, in time to say Mass, [I arrived] at San Ignacio, and we succeeded in rescuing the prisoner from death." Kino may have been able to secure fresh remounts at Guevavi, Bacoancos, San Lazaro, and Cocóspera, and the final leg to San Ignacio was only about 9 miles. But for a man of 55 riding in early May on small Spanish rock horses on rudimentary trails all day, long into the night, and likely before dawn the next morning was epic. (Kino 1948: I: 239-240).

On April 9, 1701, Kino and Manje again visited Bac. A few days earlier, the village governor and captain "of this great ranchería ... had gone out with many other natives to war against the enemies of this province of Sonora, the Hojomes, Apaches, and Janos." Added Kino:

On the 10th we rested here at San Xavier, giving various Christian instruction to the many natives who were here. We saw the good field of wheat belonging to the church, the 70 head of sheep and goats, and the cattle which had remained (for over 200 had returned to San Luys [Bacoancos] on account of the neglect of the few cowboys, especially when they had gone to eat pitahayas). Much kindness was shown us by these excellent natives. They gave us many of their provisions, many of their good fabrics and blankets of cotton, numerous baskets, buck-skins, and red feathers of the many macaws which are raised here, etc. This afternoon came the news of the victory which these Pimas had won in their war against the enemy (Kino 1948: I: 291-292).

Conspicuous by its absence is any mention by Kino or Manje of the church on which work had begun a year earlier.

1645-1711: Kino's talents

The pioneering padre of Northern Sonora and Southern Arizona was a man of many parts:

✣ Evangelist to the O'odham, baptizing over 4,500

✣ Founder of 24 missions and 11 *visitas*

✣ Farmer, rancher, and expert horseman

✣ Developer of multi-season farming and new crops, notably winter wheat

✣ Teacher of trades and ethics

✣ Architect and builder

✣ Explorer

✣ Astronomer

✣ Cartographer

✣ Linguist fluent in Italian, German, Latin, Spanish, and multiple O'odham dialects

✣ Biographer of martyr F. X. Saeta, S.J.

✣ First or early developer of the concept of letters of credit: ship paper, not bullion

✣ Peacemaker

In 1701, presumably after Kino's April visit, Fr. Francisco Gonzalvo, a Spaniard, became Bac's first resident priest. He remained until the summer of 1702 when, by Manje's account, "... he had to leave because people in the two nearby settlements of Juaxona and Tunortaca started killing the cattle and mares of his mission" (Kino 1948: I: 303; Manje 1954: 141). More likely, however, it was illness that led to his departure from Bac where, "young, enthusiastic Francisco Gonzalvo hoped and prayed for a bountiful harvest of souls. But he too reaped sickness, and in the hot, sticky month of August 1702, they carried him south through Guevavi. Weak and feverish, he lay at San Ignacio in the house of Fr. [Agustín de] Campos, his shipmate on the voyage from Spain. At four in the morning of Aug. 10 he died, having done to the end 'continuous acts of faith, hope, and charity.' He was only 29" (Kessell 1970: 32).

Kino made his tenth and last visit to Bac in September 1702. He reported beginning "the very large church of San Xavier del Bac, among the Sovaipuris" (Bolton 1948: I: 373), ignoring the fact that this task, apparently aborted, had started more than two years

previously. Gonzalvo's death had left Bac unattended by a resident priest. Kino took lamented note of this situation in 1703 and again in 1706 (Kino 1948: II: 35, 182, 185; Burrus 1961: 30).

Besides the shortage of priests, Kino's ambitious construction at other missions left Bac without a pastor and with little more than foundations for a church. During February, March, April, and part of May 1703, Kino had built new churches at Cocóspera and Remedios. He wrote that to aid in the building:

> there came from all parts a great many Pimas, from the west, the northwest, and the north, especially the numerous people of San Francisco Xavier del Bac .... These Pimas Sobaipuris of San Xavier del Bac, having returned in May to their rancherías, found that some [Piman] Indians from farther inland had eaten some of the mares of the drove belonging to the church which they had in their charge. They went in at once to punish the malefactors, beating many and taking seven children prisoners, which, to compensate for the damage these malevolent Indians had done to our drove of mares, they sent to Cocóspera and Nuestra Señora de los Dolores. They were afterwards catechized and baptized, and the two oldest girls were married, one to the captain of Cocóspera (Kino: 1948: II: 34-35).

It is now clear that no church at San Xavier grew beyond its foundations up to the time of Kino's death in Magdalena at age 65 on March 15, 1711. And for at least another ten years, there were no Spanish colonists in what is now Arizona (Officer 1987:30).

Fr. Agustín de Campos and rare *visitas*: 1702-1726

Jesuit Agustín de Campos of Mission San Ignacio became responsible for San Xavier after Gonzalvo's death in 1702. The native of Sijena, a small village in Aragón in northeastern España, became pastor of San Ignacio in 1693 at age 24 (Dobyns 1976: 182 n. 24). The *Libro de Bautismos del Partido de San Ygnacio de Caburica Núm. 1*, now in the Bancroft Library, Berkeley, Calif. (Oblasser 1960: 2-3; Dobyns 1960: 1) shows that over the next several years Campos baptized many from Bac, as on April 8, 1708; Aug. 29, 1720; Feb. 17, 1721; and Jan. 17 and 18, 1722. At Bac on March 8 and 9, 1722, Campos conducted services and baptized more people with the help of a Jesuit brother, Joseph de la Peña (Oblasser 1960: 1-2). On Feb. 24, 1724, the tireless and well-traveled Campos made another journey north, visiting "San Francisco Xavier del Bac" on March 4 and 5. At San Ignacio on Jan. 12 and 23, 1725, he baptized groups from San Xavier. And the next year he made what seems to have been his last trip to the far north. On Good Friday and Holy Saturday, April 19 and 20, he baptized at San Xavier. Almost a year later on April 17, 1727, Fr. Luis M. Gallardi, substituting for Campos at San Ignacio, baptized two children from Bac. On April 8, 1729, and twice in 1730 at San Ignacio, Campos baptized arrivals from Bac. Concludes Fr. Charles W. Polzer, the Jesuit historian:

Kino spent 24 years putting the Pimería on the map; Campos spent 43 years keeping it there (Polzer 1982: 23).

Nine new Jesuits and more brief *visitas*: 1732-1755

In 1731, a Swiss Jesuit, Philipp Segesser von Brunegg, arrived at San Ignacio, where his name is in the baptismal register at various times from Nov. 3. Segesser was joined by two more Jesuits: Ignacio Keller of Moravia and Johann Grazhofer of Austria. In May 1732, after an informal apprenticeship with veteran Jesuits on the frontier, the three priests were installed in their Pimería Alta posts by Capt. Juan Bautista de Anza the elder: Segesser at Bac, Keller at Soamca, and Grazhofer at Guevavi. On July 19, for reasons that are not clear, Segesser was back at San Ignacio where he again signed the baptismal register through March 7, 1733. The next month Segesser was at Guevavi where, on May 26, the ailing Grazhofer died in his fellow Jesuit's arms. Segesser was convinced that the Guevavi Pimans had poisoned Grazhofer, "a fact," he wrote, "which they later admitted" (Dobyns 1960: 2; Donohue 1960: 129; 1969: 68-69; Hammond 1929: 230; Kessell 1970: 42-43, 53; Oblasser 1960: 3; Roca 1967: 359 *n.* 39 and 40).

Assigned at once to Guevavi, Segesser was replaced at San Xavier by Swiss-born Fr. Gaspar Stiger, age 37. At Guevavi, Segesser managed to plant a few fruit trees, as he had done at Bac, but in a short time he, too, became deathly sick. He may have had malaria, although he was inclined to blame jealous medicine men for his problems. He was carried south to Cucurpe to recuperate for five months before returning to Guevavi (Kessell 1970: 54, 56; Roca 1967: 360 *n.* 43). At the end of July 1734, Segesser and Keller met at Soamca to celebrate the feast day of San Ignacio de Loyola, the Jesuits' founder. Says historian John Kessell:

> ... *without warning,* "*the Devil prevented the desired result, perverting to his own use the proverb, 'Mourning taketh hold of the ends of joy.' For the fathers ... beheld the feast of our Founder not with joy, but with tears.*" *The Indians of Soamca had deserted them.*

> *Segesser hastened back to Guevavi to find that his own charges had fled into the hills, driving the cattle and horses before them. At Bac, in the [temporary] absence of Stiger, the natives had simultaneously broken into the padre's house stealing everything,* "*including the new, beautiful, and precious vestments in five colors and all appurtenances which our viceroy had given to us when we were sent to these new missions.*" *Stiger hurried northward. This was rebellion.*

> *Had the Pimas of the north wished to set back the Spanish advance mightily, this was truly the time. ... But for lack of will or organization, the Pimas never followed through.*

> ... *Capt. Anza and his soldiers rushed to the scene. Already the three missionaries had begun negotiating the peaceful return of the neophytes. Once before, Fr. Segesser had brought back his flock from the mountains. Again he persuaded them to return. To San Xavier repentant natives carried back all they had stolen, though much of it was broken and torn. The cause of the flight, the padres discovered, was a rumor that the captain was coming to kill all of the Pimas. The rumor, it seemed, had been conceived and spread by malevolent Spaniards who wished to frighten the*

Indians and turn them against the missionaries. Back of it, however, the padres discerned the lurking figure of the Devil, the ubiquitous "Father of Lies."

> *From San Xavier in November [1734], Father Stiger reported each of the three missionaries "now with his own flock," though Segesser "is ill with fever; last year he almost died of it; apparently, this country is not good for his health"* (Kessell 1970: 57-58).

By now, Pimans were dying of European diseases against which they lacked immunity. The likelihood is strong that Indians had begun to associate missionaries and all Europeans as among the sources of terrible scourges taking a toll on them. The missionaries, for their part, blamed difficulties on the Devil, on poisoning, and on the medicine men ("witches") with whom they found themselves in competition (Reff 1995). Between 1733 and 1736 when he was sent to San Ignacio to replace the recalcitrant Fr. Campos, Stiger alternated between Guevavi and Bac. He apparently spent more time at Bac, but his tenure there had not been easy.

The vacancy at Bac after Stiger's transfer was partially remedied by Keller at Soamca. He promised to make frequent visits to San Xavier from his home mission, as entries in his Soamca registers confirm. In 1736 he performed baptisms at Bac on July 12-16, Dec. 15, and Christmas, and in 1737 he baptized one person on Feb. 18. Keller was relieved of the duty to visit Bac with the arrival, possibly in the spring, of German Joseph Fabier from Cucurpe east of Magdalena. Fabier, however, was gone by Aug. 10 and died Oct. 25 in San Ignacio, age 31 (Dobyns 1976: 8, 182 *n.* 38; Kessell 1970: 65 *n.* 45).

In March 1737 the Jesuits finally and forcibly removed Fr. Campos from San Ignacio. Charged with insubordination and suspected of senility, he possibly had come to identify more with Indians than Spaniards. He died four months later, age 68 (Dunne 1941: 57-58).

Alexander Rapicani, a native of the Duchy of Bremen with a Swedish mother and Neapolitan father, was assigned to Guevavi on June 1, 1737. He simultaneously assumed the responsibility for Bac. For more than a dozen years he and his successors at Guevavi served Bac as a *visita* – a mission visiting station without a resident priest. Occasionally they received an additional annual stipend of 200 pesos from the royal coffers for the extra duties (Dobyns 1976: 8; Kessell 1970: 63-65).

When Rapicani took over at Guevavi and Bac in 1737, he and Keller signed a formal transfer in the presence of Stiger. The transfer included inventories of both missions. The list for San Xavier indicated anything but wealth. There were a few tools, including four charcoal maker's axes, a carpenter's axe, and a small pruning hook. There were two adzes with their straps, a small hammer, a pair of large tongs, one file, eight chisels, one gouge, a small jack-plane, some wooden carpentry tools, and two augers, one of which was very small and broken. So too was one of two hand saws.

There were a pair of large plow points; a large copper kettle and a small one with holes; a large skillet in good condition; a decanter; a branding iron with its venting iron; six jugs; some old chests; five earthenware plates; three Puebla or *majolica* cups of tin-glazed earthenware; and two copper candlesticks with snuffers.

The furnishings for the "church," apparently nothing more than a ramada, had been badly damaged in the unpleasantness of

1734. Keller wrote that San Xavier's list of church belongings was identical to that of Guevavi, but this is unlikely. Bac's altar lamp, it was noted, had been

... completely broken to pieces when the natives sacked the house. All of these vestments and other ecclesiastical ornaments the damaged processional canopy and censer are in the possession of Capt. Anza for repair. In addition, the green maniple is missing. All of these vestments have been rather abused and the new altar cloths torn into pieces that could not be gathered up. Also one set of flowered vestments which Don Santos Fernández Ronderos, through the good offices of Don Santiago Ruiz de Ael, presented as alms, though without a frontal and linen.... Also a canvas depicting the seraphic St. Francis [of Assisi] (Kessell 1970: 198-99).

This list indicates the meagerness of Jesuit possessions, and suggests by their very listing the rarity and importance of finely woven and sewn cloth and metal tools. Worked metal, a European introduction among the Pimans, was particularly scarce on this northern frontier of Nueva España.

Bac's livestock in 1737 were listed as numbering 240 head of cattle, 150 sheep, 50 goats, 10 tame horses, four herds of a few mares, a pair of gentle mules, and no oxen (Kessell 1970: 199).

The years at San Xavier between 1737 and the Pima Rebellion of 1751 lie behind a shroud of historical uncertainty. Although Fr. Rapicani, stationed at Guevavi, was presumably responsible for San Xavier, Fr. Keller, stationed farther away at Soamca, baptized at Bac on Aug. 19, 1737. When he presented his records for inspection to Bishop of Durango Martín de Elizacochea, Keller signed himself as minister of Soamca, San Xavier del Bac, Tucsón, Opsar, Toason, Coatac, Guitoaba, and Santa Catharina. He again performed baptisms at Bac on Jan. 24 and 26, 1738, and on Aug. 28, 1743. Rapicani was often absent from San Xavier's much closer neighbor of Guevavi (Kessell 1970: 66, 68-69; Donohue 1960: 130; Oblasser 1960: 4,5).

Fr. Rapicani's successor at Guevavi and, by extension, San Xavier, was José de Torres Perea, age 28. Originally from Chalchicomula, Puebla, he arrived at Guevavi by mid-February 1741. His first wedding there on May 23 joined in holy matrimony Joseph Tutubusa, governor of Tumacácori, and Martha Tupquice of San Xavier. Ygnacio Jocumisa, governor of San Xavier, and a church assistant, Domingo Cussu, were among the witnesses (Kessell 1970: 72-74).

During his stay at Guevavi, Torres Perea baptized and blessed marriages at Bac as well as at other *visitas* and villages. Shortly before he was transferred in the spring of 1744, he penned a description of Bac (Kessell 1970: 79-80):

This Mission, which is ministered to simultaneously with that of Guebavi in Pimería Alta, is 25 leagues distant from Guebavi toward the North over a road scant in water and dangerous because of the enemy. Toward the North there no longer are Christians, but various gentile nations without the light of the Gospel nor knowledge of Christ. This Mission was founded the same year as Guebavi [sic], that is 1732 [sic] and since then until the present year 1744 shows on its baptismal register 2,142 without counting those whom other Fathers baptized before, in whose books I think they were recorded.

It is a well-populated Mission. There are more than 400 families. It is a Mission of Indians who are still mountain-dwellers, little or not

Called from far away
COLONIAL MISSIONARIES AT SAN XAVIER

Jesuits (visiting priests in italics)

Eusebio Kino, founder	1692-1702	Trento, Italy
Francisco Gonzalvo	1701-1702	Valencia, Spain
Agustín de Campos from San Ignacio	*1702-1726*	*Aragón, Spain*
Luis María Gallardi from San Ignacio	*1727-1729?*	*Sicily*
Philipp Segesser	1732	Lucerne, Switzerland
Gaspar Stiger	1733-1736	Baden, Germany
Ignacio Keller from Soamca	*1736-1743*	*Nurenberg, Germany*
Joseph Fabier	1737	Cologne, Germany
Alexander Rapicani from Guevavi	*1737-1740*	*Bremen, Germany*
José de Torres Perea from Guevavi	*1741-1744*	*Puebla, Mexico*
Ildefonso de la Peña from Guevavi	*1744*	*Mexico*
Joseph Garrucho from Guevavi	*1745-1751*	*Sardinia, Italy*
Francisco Pauer *from Guevavi*	1751 *1754-1756*	Nurenberg, Germany
Alonso Espinosa	1755-1765	Canary Islands, Spain
José Neve	1765-1767	Tlaxcala, Mexico

Franciscans

Francisco Garcés	1768-1779	Aragón, Spain
Juan P. Gorgoll	1774	??
Félix de Gamarra	1775-76	Cantabria, Spain
Juan Bautista Velderrain	1776-1790	Gipuzkoa, Spain
Joaquín Antonio Belarde	1777-1779	Cantabria, Spain
Juan Bautista Llorens	1790-1815	Valencia, Spain
Bartolomé Socies	1797-1798	Mallorca, Spain
Ignacio Ramírez y Arellano	1802-1805	Puebla, Mexico
Diego Gil	1814-	??
Gregorio Ruiz	1816-1817	Yucatán, Mexico
Juan Vaño	1819-1824	Valencia, Spain

MEXICAN-ERA FRANCISCANS

Rafael Díaz *from Cocóspera & Tucsón*	1824-1828 *1828-1834*	Cádiz, Spain *Cádiz, Spain*
Antonio González	1834-1837	Salamanca, Guanajuato
Rafael Díaz from San Ignacio	*1837-1841*	*Cádiz, Spain*
Antonio González from Oquitoa from San Ignacio	*1841-1842* *1843*	*Salamanca, Guanajuato* *Salamanca, Guanajuato*

at all amenable to the subjection of the gentle yoke of Christ. They are Christians more in name than reality. Only two Missionary Fathers [Segesser and Stiger] lived in this Mission. They bewitched one in the year 1734; they rose up and profaned the vestments and chalices. Afterwards they surrendered, and now live quietly. Since then they have been ministered to by those who are Missionaries of Guebavi (because of the scarcity of Missionaries) who cannot do what is necessary fully to teach and minister to them, because of the distance and risky terrain.

These Indians still appear to live like gentiles with the difference that in their paganism they were not baptized as they are now, without any change in their way of life. They know not how to pray, not even the "Our Father" nor the "Hail, Mary," nor to cross themselves. Many adults flee from baptism, and I have found old and very old gentiles. The majority, and nearly all, marry according to their pagan rite: they really work at avoiding being married by the Church. In this matter they hide the truth from the Missionary Fathers, telling them that they had been married by the Church by previous Fathers. This is not true, because I convince them with the marriage registers in which one does not find 30 couples married by the Church, there being more than 400 families. Yet they are not convinced. The poor Fathers work hard in this, but because the jurisdiction is large, it is not remedied according to one's wishes. Dated in Pimería Alta on the 16th day of March of 1744 (Dobyns 1976: 8-9).

Fr. Torres Perea's successor at Guevavi, who also inherited San Xavier as part of his jurisdiction, was Ildefonso de la Peña, another Mexican-born Jesuit. In mid-May 1744, Fr. Visitor Juan Antonio Balthasar, a Swiss priest, arrived on a tour of inspection. He was not pleased by what he found at Bac:

The mission of San Javier del Bac is on the fringe of the land of these [desert-dwelling Pápago] people. But it has rarely possessed a resident missionary although it is among the last of those founded through the munificence of the King. There is a bad lot of Indians here and they are poorly instructed. Moreover, there are those who abandon the mission because pueblo life is not to their liking. There are many and powerful medicine men here and they slay one another. The missionaries who have resided here [Segesser and Stiger] have become bewitched and it was necessary to withdraw them before they should die. This mission requires the assistance of soldiers who will force these Indians to live in the pueblo, since they are baptized, to labor in their fields which are fertile, to punish the medicine men and, as a warning to others, to drive forth those who are most prejudicial to the common weal of the mission. In the time of His Excellency, Viceroy [Juan Antonio de] Vizarrón [who was also archbishop of México], an order was given to exile such troublemakers to the obrajes, or workhouses, of Mexico City. But when this regime came to an end [in August 1740] the order was not carried out. In the meantime nothing was effectively done in this matter. Neither could the missionaries live in peace, nor did these medicine men leave off killing each other, nor will they bring themselves to live in a Christian manner. For this reason Your Reverence [Provincial Cristóbal Escobar y Llamas] can, for the good of souls, secure from the authorities a similar order with the same provisions, along with a firm mandate regarding its execution. You can see to it that these orders be executed without delay or exception, and thus there will be seen an improvement on all sides. Of course, I understand that the fathers themselves cannot and should not take part in such punitive measures lest they incur odium on the part of their spiritual sons. Thus some Pápagos could be incor-

porated into this mission and a famous reduction could be created here, for this center is among the most populous of all (Dunne 1957: 78-79).

Fr. Peña apparently departed Guevavi, and responsibility for San Xavier, with the father visitor's party. Except when Fr. Keller could continue to look over things from Soamca, Guevavi and Bac were left to their own devices for a year (Kessell 1976: 83-84).

The next priest assigned to Guevavi and its *visita* of San Xavier was Sardinian Joseph Garrucho. He arrived at Guevavi in May 1745. With help from Keller at Soamca, he took care of Bac and other Piman villages distant from Guevavi and Soamca till 1751. Earlier, in 1748, Fr. Visitor Carlos Rojas visited San Xavier, of which he wrote:

This mission, which has been truly unlucky, contains very many people and is almost always without a priest. It has been established for 16 years [since Segesser's arrival in 1732] and not even the first six found one priest in continual residence; the last ten years have been a matter of filling in (Rojas, quoted in Donohue 1960: 132).

In January 1751, Bavarian Jacobo Sedelmayr, a Jesuit priest at Tubutama in the Altar valley southwest of today's Nogales, wrote to his father provincial that:

Fr. Garrucho always contended there would have to be six soldiers with the missionary of San Xavier. But I argue this way: Either the Indians want to be bad or they don't. If they want to be bad, neither six nor twelve are enough. If they do not want to be bad, then two or three soldiers are plenty to maintain respect and care for his person (Sedelmayr 1751a).

In February, Sedelmayr began an inspection of the missions of the Pimería Alta, submitting his report on May 10. He visited Guevavi on Feb. 20, and soon set out

with Fr. Joseph [Garrucho] for 26 leagues to the mission of San Xavier del Bac. The padre is temporarily responsible for its administration until its own minister arrives. It is a pueblo with many houses, but of the 800 souls it is supposed to contain, hardly 100 appeared. It is still very backward, a place without a catechist, without obedience, and without any church other than a ramada and a wretched house. It is clear to see that this pueblo has been visited very little (Sedelmayr 1751c).

On May 21, Sedelmayr wrote to Fr. Balthasar that he had appointed Fr. Francisco Pauer – Franz Bauer, also sometimes spelled Paver – to San Xavier (Sedelmayr 1751b). Born in Moravia in 1721, Pauer also helped at San Ignacio. He had been at Bac hardly a half year when the Northern Pimans, i.e., the northern O'odham, staged a general uprising in November throughout the Pimería Alta. Warned by a sympathetic native governor at Bac, Pauer was able to flee with a small escort to the immediate safety of Guevavi over 50 miles south. From there he and Garrucho retreated 30 miles southeast to Soamca. Pimans killed the Jesuit missionaries at Caborca and Sonoyta, killed many other Spaniards and Indians sympathetic to the Spanish cause, and laid waste to all signs of Spanish presence at San Xavier. They completely demolished the padre's house as well as the ramada that had served as a church. "Nothing moveable ... was spared" (Dobyns 1976: 10-11; Donahue 1969: 132; Kessell 1970: 106-108).

The rebels rid their lands of foreigners, but Spanish soldiers soon arrived, and by the spring of 1752, matters were returning to the pre-rebellion status quo (Kessell 1970: 106-110).

It was 1753 before Pauer ventured north. Late in the year at San Ignacio and Soamca he baptized five villagers from San Xavier who had not joined in the rebellion. On New Year's Day 1754, the young Jesuit baptized 34 Pima children at the new presidio at Tubac, 29 of them youngsters brought by their parents from Bac. That month he took up the post at Guevavi and again found himself in charge of, although not resident in, Bac. In August Pauer visited San Xavier, reporting to Fr. Visitor General Joseph de Utrera "that the house, the church [ramada], the vestments, and all manner of livestock perished in the uprising. The mission has nothing and owes nothing. He did not even know how many families there might be, because they have not even been gathered up or brought together and therefore he was unable to get an idea." But in the same year, Bac's villagers were again entrusted with sacred vessels and vestments for their mission, even though they still lacked a resident priest. (Kessell 1970: 129, 131, 136-37; Oblasser 1960: 7-11). In early 1755 despite an illness that kept him briefly at Soamca, Pauer was again at San Xavier and baptized more children. But his duties at Bac were almost over. After over half a century, the mission would soon have a Jesuit in residence for years, not just a few brief months (Kessell 1970: 138-39).

PASTOR ALONSO ESPINOSA, THE FIRST COMPLETED CHURCH, AND THE EXPULSION OF THE JESUITS: 1755-1767

Fr. Alonso Espinosa's influence on San Xavier was the most eventful since Kino's early visits. Espinosa became the mission's most memorable resident Jesuit because he was pastor for nearly nine years – and because he built Bac's first church.

Born Feb. 1, 1720, at Las Palmas in the Grand Canary Islands off the coast of Morocco, Espinosa arrived in Yucatán and was ordained a priest at age 21. He nearly died of an illness, but on his recovery entered the Jesuit novitiate on Aug. 14, 1750. He began mission work on Aug. 15, 1752, presumably at Caborca. In April 1754 he attended a conference of missionaries, military authorities, and Pimans at San Ignacio, and the next month visited Caborca, reporting that it still seemed dangerously unsettled (some two and half years after its priest had been killed in the 1751 uprising). In mid-April 1755, Espinosa was sent to Bac, but his initial assignment was short. In mid-1756 he was in charge at Cocóspera. Pauer, for the moment, continued to add San Xavier to his duties. Finally, sometime during the last half of 1756, this novice among Pimería Alta missionaries moved in at Bac for a prolonged and eventful stay (Dobyns 1976: 14, 16; Donohue 1960: 133).

Displaying typical European disregard – if not outright disrespect – for native cultural practices, and engaging in overzealousness characteristic of youthful inexperience, Espinosa seems to have done his best to change age-old religious traditions, restraining the Pimans, says Dobyns (1976: 17), "from holding their customary dances and festivities during the fall harvest."

The response was predictable. The Pimans at Bac and to the north rose up in arms. Spanish accounts said the leader of the fighters was Gila River Chief Crow's Head (*Havañ mau' au* or, in Spanish spelling, *Jabanimó*). One report said that at Bac,

Jabanimó assaulted it with his band of rebel Pimas [in] the year 1756, and aided by the Indians of the Pueblo itself, sacked the Missionary Father's house and loyal Indians' huts. While they were so engaged, the ensign of the Royal Presidio of Tubac arrived with 15 soldiers in relief. Although the rebels received them with the greatest resistance, the latter were defeated with 15 dead and many wounded. They fled precipitously inland, leaving only three soldiers slightly wounded (Dobyns 1976: 17).

Sonoran Gov. Juan Antonio de Mendoza rode at the head of a large punitive expedition. En route toward the Gila, he picked up Espinosa at Tubac where the padre had fled, and returned him to San Xavier. Mendoza's force was unable to engage the Indians in any significant action, so returned south. At Bac the troops paused long enough for the governor to lay the cornerstone for a church. For the next five years, Espinosa would labor to bring it to completion (Kessell 1970: 141-42).

Fr. Donohue (1960: 134-35) summarizes Espinosa's tenure:

A difficult task faced the young missionary at his new post. There was a house to be built, a church constructed, mission herds to be replaced. The temper of his Indians was uncertain; while some were markedly loyal, others were suspect of being leagued with rebellious Pimas of the Gila. But he built the house, constructed the church, and enlarged the herds. His very successes made him a tempting target for the Pimas, Apaches, and Seris; their raids cut his herds from 1,000 to 200, and stole all his horses. Though the commander of the nearby presidio of Tubac, young Juan Bautista de Anza, often sent an escort of 15 soldiers to protect the mission, they were never near when most needed.

Espinosa's character revealed itself in his solution to problems. Deprived of horses, if he wished to visit yet another priest, he had to trudge 30 leagues to Guevavi .... Yet while enemies attacked and his own charges disappeared into the mountains, he rebuilt his church. During the winter of 1760, Fr. Espinosa had to admit that nearly all his Indians except the old and the sick had abandoned [Bac and its *visita* of] Tucsón ...The Indians followed the desert dweller's plan of life – valley in summer, mountains in winter. In 1762, 2,000 Sobaipuris, tired of a continual pounding from Apaches, secured Anza's approval of their migration from the valley of [the] Buenavista [today's San Pedro] to … Suamca [southeast of today's Nogales, and to] Tucsón and Bac. Espinosa did his best to make them welcome….

Circa 1760: A conjectural rendering of San Xavier's first church – a long and narrow mud adobe built by Fr. Alonso Espinosa, S.J. west of today's church. View to the north-northeast (Doug Gann, Center for Desert Archaeology).

Conjectural interior of the first church with walls of mud adobe and posts in the center of the nave to help support mid-span beams or lintels. The lintels in turn helped to carry the ceiling and roof of mesquite vigas, saguaro ribs, and hard-packed dirt (Doug Gann, Center for Desert Archaeology).

As a result of the Sobaipuris' move, Gov. [Juan Claudio de] Pineda of Sonora showed interest in Tucsón and inquired of Jesuit superiors about it. His request for information was passed on to Fr. Espinosa. Tucsón, the padre replied, had a scarcity of water, and its people showed a tendency to roam. To be able to roam freely, they had rejected his offer of stock; in this year of 1764, because of Apache raids on the herds of Bac, the offer could not be repeated.

The governor answered the letter by asking why – when they had the most likeable priest in the mission field and a captain at Tubac to punish thieves – did the natives of Bac remain the worst enemies of their own herds? The inquiry about Tucsón was not repeated.

Espinosa was elated by the completion of his church. He continued to adorn its interior, ordering from Mexico City in 1759 "a head and hands of San Xavier with a body frame resembling the statue in Vera Cruz;" in 1763, he ordered paintings for the church, and in 1765 candelabra for the altars.

But Espinosa's health was not good, and the problem deeply concerned Jesuit superiors. Already in June 1762, the superior Garrucho had reported "the Job of the missionaries" in poor health, and the next year had asked that he be replaced. Espinosa's physical ailments were complicated by the spiritual disease of scruples: excessive, worrisome torment over trifles, usually of a religious nature. In 1764, it was his eyes, and the *Visitador* Fr. [Manuel] Aguirre expressed grave concern with his problem. That winter Espinosa stayed awhile with Fr. Pauer at San Ignacio hoping to regain his strength, but he was a sick man.

The decision to replace him was probably reached in early 1765 when Aguirre visited him and registered his mission as follows:

San Xavier's patron and oldest statue, ordered in 1759 from Mexico City by Fr. Alonso Espinosa (Edward McCain).

San Xavier del Bac – Alonso Espinosa minister. Language, Pima Alta. 100 families, 29 widowed persons, 240 individuals receive the sacrament of penance, few receive that of the Eucharist; 60 are learning the catechism; in all, 270 individuals. Its visita, pueblo of Tucsón – 70 families, 58 widowed persons, 210 receive the sacrament of penance, few that of the Eucharist; 70 are learning the catechism, 220 individuals in all.

In Aguirre's estimation this was a large mission for he listed Guebavi at 100 individuals, and its *visitas* of Calabazas at 97 and Tumacácori at 164. But the Jesuit stay at Bac was drawing to a close, and the worldwide suppression of the Society of Jesus was only a few years away.

Were he to be remembered for no other reason, Alonso Espinosa's name should be emblazoned in the history of San Xavier because he built its first church. It may have left something to be desired from an engineering standpoint, but it was a real church – a substantial, flat-roofed, hall-shaped structure of sun-dried mud adobe. The church was built along a north-south axis on a considerable rise above the floodplain parallel to and west of the present church built by Franciscans late in the 1700s. The walls of Espinosa's adobe church were about three feet thick and laid on stone footings (Fontana 1973: 10j-27, 21a-45, 49-85). The base of the walls followed the contours of the gentle downward slope from southeast to northwest. No effort was made to level the site. The outer dimensions were about 23 feet by 92½ feet with about 1,800 square feet of interior floor space. The building's entrance, like that of the present church, was to the south. A sacristy may have been behind the main altar at the north end (Check 1974: 179; Robinson 1963: 38).

Not noted in the archaeological site plans on excavations here in 1958, 1967-68, and early 1972-73 was the discovery of five supports for posts in the exact center of the church. Upright posts on these pedestals supported large mesquite beams running south to north down the length of the structure. The beams provided mid-span support for shorter, smaller mesquite joists or *vigas* laid across the center beams.

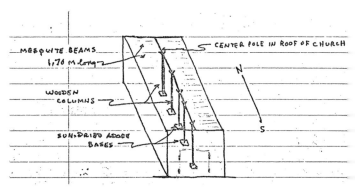

April 29, 1972: Sketch in the Field Notes of excavations at San Xavier north of the Mortuary Chapel showing five bases for posts in the exact center of the Espinosa church. Two of the posts supporting center lintels are found today in the adobe rooms east of the east tower. Adobe walls take the place of the other posts. In April 1797 (see pages 26 and 29) the west walls of two new rooms in the old church were built next to the posts – insuring that the old roof stayed in place (Fontana 1973: 84-86; Socies 1797).

The outer ends of the *vigas* rested on the upper adobe walls and their inner ends on the center beams. Resting at right angles to the *vigas* were *latillas*, or lathes, most likely the wooden ribs from saguaros. The flat roof was sealed with a thick layer of mud, possibly with straw and cow pies added to the mix to help it dry into a kind of earthen cement.

Archaeology indicated that only a small part of one wall had collapsed onto the site. There was no indication of the roof having burned or collapsed. To the contrary, all indications were that Fr. Espinosa's church had been systematically dismantled and its adobe and wood components hauled from the site for re-use elsewhere. That was indeed the case, but not till after 1797 and the completion of San Xavier's second church – the far larger and more intricate Franciscan church.

If the building of a church at San Xavier had been a momentous event during Espinosa's time, so too was the arrival under Spanish military escort in early 1762 of some 250 Sobaipuri refugees from the San Pedro Valley. The evidence is that all of them were resettled in Tucsón rather than at Bac, but Tucsón was a *visita* of San Xavier, so they became Espinosa's responsibility.

Espinosa's failing health forced him to spend part of the winter of 1764 in San Ignacio to recuperate. By Jan. 7, 1765, he was back at San Xavier, but by mid-May or perhaps a bit earlier, he was assigned a companion, Fr. José Neve, 35, a Jesuit born in Tlaxcala east of Mexico City whose initial brief assignment in the Pimería Alta had been at Atil. Neve found Espinosa bedridden and unable to move (Dobyns 1976: 23-24).

San Xavier's church property was formally transferred from Espinosa to Neve on June 16 with Pauer as a witness. The list of goods was far more extensive than that of June 1, 1737. In addition to a generous supply of vestments and church cloths, including a cope of Persian silk and six Brittany altar cloths with lace and two without lace, there was "1 statue of San Xavier with cassock of ribbed silk. Surplice of cambric and another of Brittany and] 2 shirts of Brittany for the saint" – the same statue ordered by Espinosa in 1759 and which now graces the central niche of the main altar (Ahlborn 1974: front cover, 92-93). There were also a copper baptismal font, doubtless the same one bearing the IHS Jesuit monogram in today's baptistery; four chalices; a pair of copper hand bells; a silver censer with its silver incense boat and spoon; a gilded silver monstrance; a gilded tabernacle with its key; a half dozen metal wall candle holders; a missal stand varnished with vermilion; three birettas; and three baptismal shells, "1 silver, 2 from the sea [Kino's abalone shells?], and 1 baptismal cap" (Kessell 1970: 203-04).

There were also three pictures, either prints or paintings: one of Our Lady of Refuge, one of San José, and a third of San Xavier from the waist up." And there was "1 image of the Sorrowing Mother with her aureole and dagger of silver, her satin dress and blue taffeta mantle with silver galloon" – the lovely image now in the bottom niche of the east wall of the east transept (Ahlborn 1974: 204-05; Kessell 1970: 204).

The "furnishings of the house" included chisels, planes, adzes, axes, sawbucks, a trowel, a whipsaw, shovels, augers, a hoe, a crowbar, a pair of branding irons with the venting iron, and reaping hooks. There were a half dozen pewter plates, 14 cups and two saucers, six spoons and seven forks, two chocolate pots, three small kettles (one bottomless), a pair of candlesticks with snuffers, a table cloth with six napkins, and "3 poor tables; 6 worse chairs" (Kessell 1970: 204-05).

The mission's larder was in good shape: 334 head of branded and 125 head of unbranded cattle; 536 head of sheep; 14 yokes of gentle oxen; 24 saddle- and halter-broken horses; 14 colts; 17 branded fillies; 19 mules (some broken and some not); and 100 brood mares with four stud horses and two stud burros. "In addition to what has been stated, the mission has what is necessary, even to adequate crops of wheat and maize. Tallow, lard, candles, and soap in good supply, all kinds. There is also a field planted with wheat, another with maize, and another various legumes, such as vetch, lentils, chickpeas, etc." (Kessell 1970: 204-05).

La Dolorosa – Our Mother of Sorrows – was listed in the June 1765 inventory when Fr. Espinosa stepped down as pastor. The image is today the central focus of the east transept and enjoys regular changes of dress thanks to the Ladies Guild (Edward McCain).

The hammered copper baptismal font from San Xavier's first church nested in a late 1700s Franciscan stand of brick, lime plaster, gesso, and paint that today is nearly gone (Edward McCain).

The copper lid of the font with the IHS monogram and a cross above the ba of the H – the Jesuit insignia. Remnants of painted enamel still cover muc of the lid (Edward McCain).

Neve was able to nurse Bac's former pastor to sufficient health so that he could be taken in October to San Ignacio. Neve likely accompanied him. By February 1766, Espinosa was well enough to move to an assignment at Caborca, and Neve had meantime returned to Bac. Apaches in February or March slipped behind troops supported by 30 O'odham auxiliaries, rustling 300 head of cattle from San Xavier. This time, however, a courageous corporal and the few soldiers stationed at Bac rode off in hot pursuit. To the amazement and joy of Neve, they returned driving the herd before them (Kessell 1970: 173).

Neve was stationed there at the end of July 1767 when all the Pimería Alta Jesuits got the call to report to the mission headquarter at Tubutama. Once there, Neve and his fellow Jesuits were led awa under arrest by military guard to Matapé in southern Sonora. From there, those who survived would eventually be taken to Vera Cruz for transport to Spain. King Carlos III had followed the preceden set by France and Portugal in ordering that all Jesuits be removed from his overseas possessions. After almost 75 years, Bac's Jesuit era had come to an end (Dobyns 1976: 24; Kessell 1970: 182-86).

THREE FRANCISCAN GIANTS – FRIARS GARCÉS, VELDERRAIN, AND LLORENS: 1768 TO 1815

Francisco Garcés, explorer and martyr: 1768-1779

Missionaries of the Order of Friars Minor headquartered at the Colegio de la Santa Cruz in Querétaro replaced the expelled Jesuits in the Pimería Alta. The Franciscan who drew the San Xavier assignment, and who arrived here on June 29, 1768 after Bac had not seen a priest for nearly a year, was "…a man 30 years old, successful only at singing in a choir and luring little boys to confession with candy bribes. If not exactly a *tabula rasa*, he was at least a person altogether uncorrupted by experience. Well, perhaps that was his trump: he had so little to unlearn and nowhere to grow but up" (Holterman 1973: 55; see Grijalva 1768 for the date of arrival).

His name was Fr. Francisco Hermenegildo Garcés, and he was the first of three Franciscans at Bac over the next 47 years who left major legacies in the history of Arizona and the Southwest. Garcés, born in Aragón near Zaragoza in northeastern Spain on April 12, 1738, arrived in Nueva España in 1763. At the Colegio de la Santa Cruz northwest of Mexico City he was regarded as simple and artless – known among his fellow friars as the "Children's Priest" (Dobyns 1976: 26).

By the time the Franciscans arrived in their new posts in the Pimería Alta, the Spanish government had changed the rules.

Mission temporalities – the worldly properties of the church – had been turned over to the care of civil comissioners. Missionaries no longer could direct the labor of Indians in support of the mission and were expected to live solely from a stipend, usually about 300 pesos a year, provided from the royal treasury. Says historian Kieran McCarty, himself a Franciscan:

Colegio de la Santa Cruz in Querétaro in central Mexico – headquarters for almost all of the Franciscans in the Pimería Alta
(Zephyrin Engelhardt, O.F.M. – "Franciscans in Arizona," 1899).

The civil commissioner was to turn over to the missionary upon his arrival only those items of mission property pertinent to implementing that role [spiritual chaplain to the mission effort]: the missionary's residence with its effects and the mission church with its effects ….with his [royal stipend] the missionary was to clothe himself, buy his food from the produce of his own mission, and pay whatever Indian help he needed to establish some kind of household. Out of this stipend he was to maintain both church and house by way of needed furnishings and repairs. In other words, once the church and house were turned over to the missionary by formal inventory, the missionary was already paid in full for all of his future years of service to that mission, as far as the civil commissioner and the possessions of the mission were concerned. Meanwhile, the coveted mission lands with their stock and agricultural products, as well as the even more coveted commodity of Indian labor, were to be represented as belonging to the Indians but in actuality were to subserve the royal coffers through the agency of the civil commissioner (McCarty 1981: 53-54).

At Bac, Civil Commissioner Andrés Grijalva made a careful inventory on June 29, 1768 before turning some of the property over to Garcés. His list is highly informative:

The undersigned civil commissioner, Don Andrés Grijalva, arrived in the village of San Xavier del Bac because of the commission given me to inventory the jewels of the church, sacristy, and convent, and to deliver them to the Rev. Fr. Friar Francisco Garcés. And finding myself in the church and acting in accordance with said letter, I proceeded in the presence of the two justices, the governor, and mayor (alcalde) of this village to make the inventory as follows:

First, the church with 3 altar tables. The main altar is comprised of a small sculptured tabernacle of gilded wood. Also a sculptured image of San Francisco Xavier including head, arms, and hands with cassock, biretta of corded silk fabric, shirt and rochet of linen of Brittania, and damask stole. Also, an old damask curtain. Also, two medium-sized paintings in gilded frames of the Virgen and San José. Also, a small one of San Francisco Xavier in a gilded frame. Also, 4 engravings [prints] on paper.

On the second altar there is a beautiful image of La Dolorosa clothed in a brocaded dress and blue cloak of ribbed silk fabric enhanced with a band of silver lace, coronet, batiste lace, and blouse of linen of Brittania. Also a silk scarf. Also, a dagger with dagger handle with a half shell of silver. Also a silver halo with its rays. Also, a silver rosary, another of black glass beads decorated with silver with a small silver cross. Also, some silver bracelets and black glass beads. Also, some silver earrings chased with gems and a strand of pearls. Also, a strand of silver. Also, a fabric ribbon with silver flowers. Also, two small bells to call the people.

On the third altar there are 4 prints on paper. Also, a curtain of green-corded silk fabric. Also, six metal wall candlesticks.

The sacristy has an old table and some prints on paper. Also, two little metal bells and a metal box for the hosts. Also, a dish, wine vessels for Mass, and a little silver bell. Also, a censer and incense boat with a silver chain. Also, a gilded silver monstrance. Also, some curtains of the Lord. 4 silver chalices, two of them broken. Also, a silver baptismal shell. Also, 3 altar stones. Also, three old missals, some curtains with flowers, and gold galloon. Also, 2 administration manuals. Also, a square [Indian-made] basket holding a rochet of Dutch linen, a velvet bonnet, a silk stole with silver galloon, and some spangles with which it is decorated. Also, three cinctures and 3 palls. Also, a red damask chasuble and gold galloon. Also, an old chasuble with veil and a damask corporal bag. Also, a black cape and another one with flowers. Also, another chasuble with a veil of brocade and gold galloon. Also, another one of brocade with the same. Also, another with the same, old, of red taffeta, and another one of corded silk fabric with silk galloon, another one of white damask and gold galloon. Also, 6 antependia which correspond. Another one of painted cloth. Also, a surplice. Also, 4 altarcloths. Also, 4 albs. Also, a small metal cross. Also, some altarcloths. Also, 6 purificators, 4 amices, 3 wash stands. 5 with their altar. 6 plain corporals. Palls: 5. A carpet. Also, a bag in which the amice is kept. Also, a shirt of San Francisco. Also, 6 gilded and silvered bouquets with their wooden vases. Also, a processional cross and wooden processional candle holders. Also, a painted canvas throne for the Blessed Sacrament. Also, a brass baptismal font, two holy water buckets, glass chrismatories with wooden box. Also, 3 boxes without a lock for the church vestments. Also, 6 silvered candlesticks and two older ones. Also, 2 of copper. Also, a wooden lectern. Also, a cambric cloth with lace of Milan and embroidered in gold, which belongs to San Francisco. Also, another small missal. Also, two books of baptisms, marriages, and burials, which begin in the year 1755.

Also, the convent with two rooms, storeroom, kitchen, and bakery [probably the adobe northeast of the church as seen in photos at least as late as 1880]. *Also, 3 tables, a large one and the 3 others as old as the doors. Also, two old chairs. Also, ten prints on paper. Also, a hide trunk lined with woven mat, another small traveling one for the chocolate. Also, 22 small and large books and old. Also, 10 forks and spoons with one of them broken. 4 metal dishes, two of pewter and very, very old. 7 dishes of Chinese porcelain, 7 cups from Puebla, 5 small cups from Puebla, half a leather trunk, two small vials of glass, 3 small tin pots, two older ones. A vial, 3 vessels, and a small one. Also, a crystal vase, a metal basin, a leather cot and another very old one of coarse brown linen, both without awnings* [and on the margin: *and useless because they are torn*]. *2 old copper kettles. Also, two old machetes to chop meat. Also, a small, old copper cauldron. Also, two old iron pans. Also, some tablecloths, 1 brass mortar, a small metal shaker, 2 chocolate jugs, an old, broken, and useless small copper pot. Also, a small drill, a chisel, and a hammer. Also an old clock taken to pieces. Also, a trough. Also, a writing desk with two keys. A necklace of false pearls, 4 candles, a salt shaker, a barrel, a blued axe.*

With which the faithful inventory of the Mission of San Xavier del Bac was finished, with the commission that has been conferred on me. I authorize it on the said day, month and year, before the undersigned witnesses present, with whom I proceed from lack of a public and royal notary whom there is not in the conditions stipulated by law, and in this common paper because the sealed one has not yet been introduced. I give true testimony of all.

Andrés Grijalva

The undersigned certified having received all that is underwritten, as minister for His Majesty, and which belongs to this Mission of San Xavier del Vac. And so that it be recorded I sign it on the said day, month and year, and also for the San Ignacio Governor and the son Manuel the Mayor, who do not know how to write.

Friar Francisco Garcés, Minister for His Majesty

Grijalva had also taken an inventory of agricultural products and livestock late in the summer of 1767 soon after the Jesuits had departed. When he made a similar accounting in October 1768, some three-quarters of the earlier amount remained. The 30 bushels of corn noted in 1767 were gone in 1768. Cattle were fewer, but the 20 saddle horses increased to 24. And in comparing the material possessions in 1765 versus 1768, San Xavier had not fared too badly (McCarty 1981: 56).

Garcés had been at Bac a month when he wrote to Capt. Juan Bautista de Anza at Tubac to tell him that a room was available for him, and to Gov. Pineda to report that the missions of San Xavier and Tucsón were quiet, and that the "Indians are content to see our King wants them as people and not as slaves" (Dobyns 1976: 27).

In June 1768, San Xavier was still the northernmost outpost of the Spanish empire in the Pimería. No other missions or presidios stood between it and the hostile Apaches. But Garcés had a serious case of wanderlust. He had been at his mission just two months when he set out on Aug. 29 for a three-day tour of Pápago country and that of the Gila River Pimas accompanied only by a parishioner and four Pápagos as guides. He became seriously ill when he returned to Bac and had to be taken to Guevavi to recuperate. While at Guevavi, on Oct. 2, Apaches "descended on San Xavier, killed the Indian governor, made captives of two soldiers, pillaged the mission and made off with the livestock." When Garcés returned to his mud adobe church he "immediately had the mission repaired" (Holterman 1973: 76, 80-81; Kessell 1976: 46-48).

The next Apache attack, by some 30 warriors in a daylight raid, came on Feb. 20, 1769 when Garcés was home. "While most of the attackers kept Fr. Garcés and the mission guard pinned down in the center of the village with a hail of arrows, others got off with most of the livestock. Before they withdrew, 'they shot many arrows at the door of the church.' They also fired arrows at a corner of the house where the soldier escort, probably no more than two or three men, had gone for protection. After a third raid on March 3, *Comisario* Andrés Grijalva reported the mission reduced to only 40 cattle and seven horses" (Holterman 1973: 83; Kessell 1976: 49-50).

Bac's peripatetic minister left again in March 1769 to serve as chaplain for a punitive expedition to the San Pedro Valley in search of Apaches. Soon after, in April and again in late June or early July, Apaches ran off more of San Xavier's livestock (Holterman 1973: 84-86). If there was any good news for Garcés in 1769, it was that a new Spanish decree issued in June again entrusted all temporal goods of the Pimería Alta missions to the Queretaran friars, effectively ending the civil commissioner system (McCarty 1981: 101).

Cal N. Peters painting: "Departure of Anza's second California expedition, Tubac, October 1775" (Tubac Presidio State Historic Park).

Off again, this time on a trek to the Gila from Oct. 19 to Nov. 2, 1770, Garcés left no replacement at Bac, and none when he went to Tumacácori for a protracted stay at the end of the month (Holterman 1973: 99, 103-04).

Apaches staged a sixth raid on Feb. 2, 1771, killing two villagers, stealing livestock and oxen, and wantonly slaughtering 350 head of smaller animals, probably goats and sheep. Such attackers strained the limits of Christian love and charity (Holterman 1973: 108-09).

Juan Bautista de Anza depicted by Bill Yslas leads a procession of re-enactors from the Anza Trail Color Guard. Islas is also a volunteer soldier at today's partial reconstruction of the Presidio San Agustín del Tucsón, founded 1775 (Jim Rogers).

From Aug. 8 to Oct. 26, 1771, Garcés went on his sixth trip, another extended journey toward the west. This time, however, there was presumably a friar filling in for him, although who it might have been is not known (Holterman 1973: 116, 167, 182).

In 1772, Friar Antonio María de los Reyes, who in 1782 became the first bishop of Sonora, described Bac – which he had probably never visited – in a report:

> The village of San Xavier at Bac is situated on open ground with an abundance of water and good land where the Indians cultivate a few small fields of wheat, Indian corn, and other crops. The church [Espinosa's flat-roofed adobe] is of medium capacity, adorned with two side chapels [side altars in the nave] with paintings in gilded frames. In the sacristy are four chalices, two of which are unserviceable, a pyx, a censer, dish and cruets, a baptismal shell, all of silver, four sets of vestments of various colors, with other ornaments for the altar and divine services – all very poor. According to the census book, which I have here before me, there are 48 married couples, seven widowers, 12 widows, 26 orphans, the number of souls in all 270 (Reyes 1772: 48-49).

Garcés was away from Jan. 8 to July 10, 1774 on the Anza expedition to California. Fr. Juan P. Gorgoll. a "tall, red-faced" friar "with a small wart on his nose" substituted for him at Bac. Gorgoll had arrived in the Pimería Alta in 1771, and rode from Caborca to fill in. During his temporary charge at San Xavier and its *visita* of Tucsón, Fr. Visitor Antonio Ramos and the visitation's secretary, Fr. José Matías Moreno, visited both villages. At Bac on June 8, they counted 161 residents: 38 married couples, 17 widowers, seven widows, nine boys over 12 years old, 30 boys of minor age, seven girls over 12, and 14 of minor age. Included was one gentile being readied for baptism. All were Indians (Baldonado 1959: 23; Dobyns 1959: 19; Holterman 1973: 197, 225; Kessell 1976: 72, 95).

Gorgoll complained to the Visitor that in Bac and Tucsón:

> …the Indians in these pueblos very often absent themselves wandering about through the various missions in search of food. There are two causes for this: the first, and principal one, is their laziness and indolence, which is common to every Indian. And the second cause is that the lands of these pueblos yield very little. Even though at planting time they get crops in the ground, then, as they are accustomed to wander,

they leave them unattended. Finally they return, each getting but little from a limited harvest" (Baldonado 1959: 24).

Garcés was off again with Anza to California in 1775-76, his eighth trip. He departed Bac on Oct. 25, leaving in charge Friar Félix de Gamarra, a Cantabrian born in 1747. Garcés returned to San Xavier on Sept. 17, 1776 after travels to central California, the Havasupai village deep in the western Grand Canyon, and Oraibi on the Hopi mesas. There he was refused entry on a notable day in American history: July 4, 1776 (Garcés 1900: I: 63-64, II: 392-403, 440; Kessell 1976: 111).

✚ ✚ ✚

J. B. de Velderrain begins the new church: 1779-1790

Sometime toward the end of 1776, "A long, tall Basque with black hair and grayish eyes, *ojos gatos* as the Spanish said, took refuge at Tumacácori .... Only 29, Fray Juan Bautista de Velderrain was from [Zizurkil in the Basque province of Gipuzkua] just off the heavily traveled highway leading south-southwest from the north coast port of San Sebastián. In the port city he had taken his first vows in 1763, and not six years after at the convento grande in Vitoria volunteered, though still a sub-deacon, for the mission of 1769 to the college of Querétaro. By 1773 he was missionary to the problem Pimas Bajos of Tecoripa and Suaqui, where three years had made him a veteran" (Garate n.d.; Kessell 1976: 127).

The sixth of eight children of Andoniz de Velderrain Igarza and Magdalena de Ubillos, Velderrain was to be the second of the great Franciscans at Bac in the nearly half century after the Jesuit expulsion. In southern Sonora he put his time to good use at Suaqui by overseeing construction of a new church. Although Spaniards Pedro Faxalde and Pedro Aldaco were the architect and master carpenter, the labor was performed by the Sibúbapas (Lower Pimas) and Velderrain himself. Work got underway on May 14, 1774, and 11 days later the Indians had almost finished a kiln for firing 3,000 adobes already on hand. This was the extra step beyond the sun-dried mud adobe of most Jesuit construction to the longer-lasting fired or burnt adobe used often by the Franciscans. Because the Pimas could not attend to their crops while work was underway, Velderrain paid them in wheat, corn, cigarettes, and raw sugar. "I assure you," the friar wrote a Spanish official, "these people work not like Indians nor even like the Spanish settlers of this land, but more like laborers from our own homeland" (Garate n.d.; McCarty 1976: 66-69). Added Velderrain:

> *I continue to labor for God and king, at times playing the role of governor of this village, at times constable, at times guest master, at times quartermaster, at times master builder, at times common laborer. I have to be everywhere at once and with everyone. I almost forget that I am a priest, except when I am saying Mass or teaching Christian doctrine. … during the one day I was not able to work at their side, my workers accomplished very little* (McCarty 1976: 68).

The Suaqui church completed, Velderrain left the Pimería Baja in August for Tumacácori, where he lingered only briefly. He was assigned to San Xavier to help Garcés or, more properly, become his permanent fill-in when the explorer friar was

on the road. In September 1776, Garcés had been back at Bac only a week after his epic journey when he was writing a letter from Tumacácori. In a letter to the guardian of the Querétaro college on Christmas 1776, Garcés is clear that Velderrain had already arrived at San Xavier. To free him to write the finished version of the diary of his 1775-76 travels, Garcés asked that yet another priest be sent so Velderrain would have a companion. His immediate superior responded by sending Fr. Joaquín Antonio Belarde. Both Velderrain and Belarde, said Garcés, "are good religious" (Holterman 1973: 383-84).

Both were at San Xavier when Garcés temporarily retired to Tubutama in late 1776 and early 1777 to collect his thoughts on the second Anza expedition to California on which he had served for part of the way. By Jan. 3, 1777, Fray Félix de Gamarra, who had substituted for Garcés at Bac in 1775-76, had left for Tumacácori and Atil (Holterman 1973: 394).

Although the documentary record is thin, Fr. Garcés was not quite done with San Xavier. On Jan. 21 and Feb. 19, 1777, he wrote letters from the Tucsón *visita*. Historian Jack Holterman (1973: 407) writes that "We have no way of knowing just when Francisco Garcés terminated his long service at San Xavier and Tucsón. We may presume he spent much of … 1778 at both these outposts and concluded his life there sometime in 1779." By March 1779, the well-traveled padre was at Atil making preparations for a new venture among the Quechans at Yuma, a missionary effort destined to end there in his violent death – as well as in that of three other friars and many Spaniards – on July 19, 1781 (Bringas 1977: 81, 83 *n.* 68, 85-87, 96-97, 100-106; Forbes 1965: 185-201; McCarty 1975; Roca 1967: 345 *n.* 24-27).

What was the daily routine for the Northern Pimans – the O'odham – living at Bac in the 1770s? In 1769, Fr. Mariano Antonio de Buena y Alcalde, Fr. President of the Franciscans' missions in Sonora, set forth a plan – one borrowed from an earlier system used in Franciscan missions in Texas and Coahuila – that was approved by Spanish Visitor General José de Gálvez. On paper, at least, it looked like this:

> *At sunrise every morning, the mission bell would announce Mass. An elderly Indian called the mador and two fiscales [assistants] went through the village waking up all the children and unmarried neophytes to attend Mass, prayers, and the catechism that were recited in unison and in Spanish. At sunset the Doctrina and prayers were repeated in the plaza in front of the church. The rosary was recited with the Salve Regina and the Gloria al Padre …. On Sundays and holy days the mador and fiscales would insist that everyone attend Mass properly washed, combed and dressed.*
>
> *High Mass was sung by a choir of four to six Indian men or women to the accompaniment of an Indian orchestra of harps and violins. During Lent everyone was supposed to assist daily at Mass and the Spanish prayers. The priest would give instruction in the Indian language, with an added instruction on Sunday evenings. Special services were held during Holy Week according to the regular Roman liturgy with probably some of the other devotions or rituals customary in Spanish countries. The problems of administering confession and communion were unusually difficult. But at the regular missions most of the Indians were at least able to confess in Spanish. On special feast days, notably those of Mary, processions were organized and the rosary was recited or chanted.*

A certain degree of elective self-government was in force. Once a year, in the presence of their padre, the mission Indians elected a chief or mayor or governor and also various subordinate alcaldes. ... These officials received places of honor in church. Their special duty was to superintend the farming and the cattle, and no doubt to help enforce law and order.

The work of the mission was either communal or individual. In planting time all the Indians assembled to receive their shares of seed from the friar, whereas from their chief or an alcalde they checked out on loan the tools, yokes, and other equipment they might need. The Indians were free to work for the mission or for themselves. Those who worked to support themselves had more independence but not necessarily greater security. Those who worked for the mission stored their crops in the community warehouse, from which they drew food and clothing for themselves and their families. If the mission had more priests than one ... sometimes the extra priest would superintend and assist the laborers; sometimes, however, one of the [Spanish] colonists was hired as a straw boss [mayordomo]. The sick, the aged, and the orphans received a sustenance gratis (Holterman 1973: 176-77).

Fray Joaquín Belarde, the blue-eyed, brown-haired Basque who was sent to San Xavier in late 1776 as an assistant to Velderrain, had arrived in Sonora in 1773. He was first stationed among the Seri Indians at Pitic and in 1775 substituted for Fr. Pedro Font – a member of the Anza expedition of 1775-76 – in the Pimería Baja at San José de Pimas. This 5'-6" friar was not at San Xavier long. By September 1777 he was the assistant to Fray Pedro de Arriquibar, another Basque, at Tumacácori. Belarde left Tumacácori for San Xavier once more in August 1779, but again not for long. He died in the mining community of Cieneguilla, Sonora on March 5, 1781, age 35 (Dobyns 1976: 36-38; Kessell 1976: 111, 133-34).

Precisely when Fr. Velderrain, the builder of the church at Suaqui, began work on the second – and present – church at San Xavier remains uncertain. Till his departure from Bac and Tucsón in 1779, Garcés made no mention of any new church, at least not among the small number of documents found generated by him after 1776. Historian Kieran McCarty (1976: 65) suggests that since Velderrain is known to have arrived at San Xavier late in 1776 and is known to have begun construction of the new church, he probably began "the planning, contracting, and building" between 1776 and 1783. That the work wasn't under way by May 1780 is suggested by the report made that year by engineer Gerónimo de la Rocha, who was on a tour of inspection of Spain's northern frontier. If construction had begun, he almost surely would have mentioned it. He wrote, however:

... We remained at San Xavier three days [May 19-21] .... This pueblo of San Xavier forms a square with its houses, and lacks only a few small gates to be entirely enclosed. At the four corners they are in the process of building four rounded defense towers with gun ports facing in every direction. Even though it is in a spacious valley, the pueblo is placed squarely in the middle of the low hills known as the badlands of San Xavier. Using the hills as shelter, the Apaches appear suddenly from behind them.

This mission is enjoying good progress in the cultivation of its fertile fields. Its population is composed of a goodly number of Pima Indians, along with some white settlers [Spaniards brought in by Velderrain

as builders?]. I consider it as certainly one of the more flourishing villages (Rocha y Figueroa 1780).

This description does not account for the Franciscan configuration of San Xavier, although in time the church came to form the north side of a plaza otherwise enclosed by rectangular-shaped adobe row houses (see the 1849 drawing by H.M.T. Powell on page 33). There is no hint in Powell's drawing nor in any archaeology thus far carried out at San Xavier of the four rounded towers described by Rocha.

The date nearly always given for the beginning of the Franciscan church is 1783. According to oral tradition, the church took 14 years to build, and multiple evidence confirms that construction ended in 1797. The 14 years is first cited by Vicar Apostolic Jean B. Salpointe, and even he hedged the guess by saying that "*if* [italics mine] the tradition be right about the time spent for the building of the church," its foundations would have been laid in 1783" (Salpointe 1880: 8; 1898: 143). In Tubutama in the Altar valley 100 miles to the south-southwest, Fr. Antonio Barbastro completed his ornate but smaller church in 1783 when it was the Franciscan headquarters for the Pimería Alta. Some of its skilled workers may have then been able to move to San Xavier (Barbastro 1971: 75).

Whenever construction began, it could have been none too soon. The bases of the mud adobe walls of Fr. Espinosa's church were spalling away through erosion produced by salts in the clay. To remedy this, and as revealed through archaeology beginning in 1958, the Franciscans built a low buttress of stones set in lime mortar all along the outer adobe walls to reinforce them. (Cheek 1974: 178-183; Robinson 1963: 40).

In the meantime, and perhaps working under the direction of Spanish architect (*maestro albañil*) Ygnacio Gauna, the O'odham at Bac excavated trenches for footings; gathered large volcanic rocks for the foundations and for the infill of the brick-veneer walls; built a lime kiln; excavated lime and burned and slaked it; excavated clay for adobes that were molded to shape before being fired into bricks; cut and hauled wood needed for firing lime and bricks; hauled water for slaking the lime and for mixing lime mortar; cut and hauled wood for doors, door frames, and lintels for windows as well as for the pulpit, altar railings, and window spindles; prepared whitewash; and did all those hundreds of laborious tasks without which such a monument would have been impossible. As Fr. Velderrain had said of the lower Pimans, they are "more like laborers from our own homeland [Spain]" (Fontana 1996a: 365-384).

Carlos III on the 1783 peso – 8 reales – minted in Mexico City
(coins.sudukuone.com).

The east wall of the choir loft: never finished despite depicting the first Franciscan – San Francisco de Asís in his Fiery Chariot (Edward McCain).

Fr. Barbastro, the builder at Tubutama, was even more enthusiastic about the Pimans. He wrote of them in 1793:

> *During the time that my Colegio [de la Santa Cruz in Querétaro] has governed these missions they introduced the use of lime mortar and brick with which the Indians were previously unacquainted, and with these materials they raised from the foundations the churches of Pitiqui[to], San Ignacio, Sáric, and Tubutama, always keeping the sword in one hand to fight the enemy* [Apaches and apostate O'odham] *and the trowel in the other. They constructed with them the most beautiful arches which, like something never before seen, caused admiration not only* [among northern O'odham] *but in all of Sonora and roused the praises of God. All of them have been praised, and at last we hope to see finished ... the church which they are building in the Mission of San Xavier del Bac. That is the northernmost village of the Christian world and everyone thinks it rivals the most beautiful churches in México. In this country it should rightly be termed "astounding"* (Fontana 1995: 31).

Velderrain borrowed 7,000 pesos for construction of the church, an amount he optimistically thought would be large enough to insure its completion (Franciscans then received about 350 pesos a year from the royal treasury as their salary). He must have been an able salesman, for all the good padre had to offer as collateral to his creditor, Don Antonio Herreros, were crops of wheat as yet unplanted (Iturralde 1795).

By mid-1788 at San Xavier, the "overall structure was finished" (McCarty 1977a: 45). But less than two years later on May 2, 1790 with detailing and other work far from finished, Fr. Velderrain died at Bac "from a vomiting of blood" (Bringas 1977: 63 *n.* 36). He may be buried beneath the sanctuary he set in place.

J.B. Llorens completes San Xavier: 1790-1815

The third of the great first Franciscans and the pastor on whose shoulders fell the task of finishing the job so well begun was Fr. Juan Bautista Llorens. "Swarthy" and "bushy-browed," Llorens was from Valencia in Spain. He arrived in Nueva España in 1785 and spent most of his time from 1787 to 1790 in the Pimería Alta at Atil, going from there to Bac (Bringas 1977: 66 *n.* 40; Dobyns 1976: 41; Kessell 1976: 185).

With the church substantially constructed, it was up to Llorens to see to the decoration of its interior and to all the minute detail of its finishing. But inflation in Europe led to restricted funding

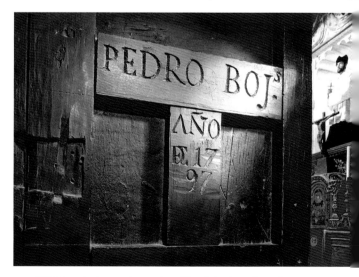

1797 inscription on the sacristy side of the doors from the sanctuary. Bojorques was possibly a foreman or master carpenter (Edward McCain).

And a 1792 change in colonial policy meant missionaries could no longer depend on income from mission lands. "As the mission Indians' living standards presumably rose, mission building income fell just when inflation caused construction contracts to rise" (Dobyns 1976: 41). Moreover, skilled artisans brought up from central Nueva España had their salaries doubled because of the hazards – the Apaches. As a result, Capt. José Zúñiga of Tucsón reported in August 1804 that for San Xavier, "a conservative estimate of the building expenses to date would be 40,000 pesos" – about $1.2 million today (McCarty 1977b: 49).

San Xavier's sculptor(s) and painter(s) remain unknown, but the probability is strong they came from the environs of the Franciscan college in Querétaro where similar Baroque decoration was still in vogue in the mid-1700s and where the friars would have had good contacts. Sometime between 1911 when he arrived at San Xavier and 1930, Fr. Bonaventure Oblasser interviewed an elderly Sobaipuri woman who lived at Bac, Carnacion (Encarnación) Anton. She told him, he wrote, that her grandfather and her grandmother on her father's side of the family had helped build the church. She also said:

> The man who did all of the interior decoration was Vishak Namkan (The One Who Meets the Chicken Hawk). He was a Mexican. He alone did all that work [painting]. The Indians would help to bring him things. He would stay way up the wall, standing on the cornice, and work for hours. The church looked very beautiful at that time. On one occasion this artist left for Caborca and never returned. That is why some of the work in the church is unfinished (Oblasser 1930-31; Rohder 1982: 14, 16).

Because of costs beyond expectations, the east bell tower was never completed. Lacking a dome and lantern and even upper plaster for nearly 110 years, the tower has given rise to all manner of latter-day folk explanations. One holds that various people (from Fr. Kino to the architect or an Indian worker) fell from the tower and thus frightened others off the job. Another story is that by leaving the church unfinished the friars and Indians avoided having to pay taxes to the Crown. But the Crown paid missionaries regardless of church conditions, and Indians had to pay taxes only after churches were removed from the control of the missionaries and turned over to secular clergy. That would take place after the missionaries had completed their goal of Christianizing and otherwise assimilating Indians into Spanish culture. Indians would then become subjects of Nueva España and liable for taxes. But this had nothing to do with the structural status of the church.

The east bell tower was left unfinished for one reason only: the lack of more money.

Friar Bartolomé Socics, born in Mallorca, appears in the mission registers of both Atil and Tubutama in 1791 but was stationed at Aconchi on the Río Sonora on Feb. 1, 1797 when he set out for his new assignment as an assistant to Llorens. After passing through Arizpe, Cocóspera, and Tumacácori, he arrived at Bac

Unfinished: "El Bautismo de Jésus" in the baptistery (Edward McCain).

The baptistery dado or wainscot: partially complete (Edward McCain).

on Feb. 20 (Kessell 1976: 191; McCarty 1977a: 46; Roca 1967: 375 *n.* 52; Socies 1797). In a letter to Fr. Diego Bringas on April 28, 1797, Socies expressed his ambivalence about the magnificent new church just completed at Bac. True to his Franciscan roots, he told Bringas he had no interest in temporal matters, and that:

> Some temporal and material affairs [here] *seem to me to be excessive, although if one looks at it from another viewpoint, they may seem to be proper .... However, I have no talent for many things, including anything out of the ordinary in material and temporal matters .... This church seems good to me, because, even though it is out of the ordinary, after all, it does serve the divine cult and is God's house. However, the spiritual church of Aconchi seems better to me and suits me much more. ... to arrange or to wish for the Indians and the Mission to have extraordinary things, superfluous ones, is dangerous and not fitting* (Socies 1797).

Socies was pleased, however, by an addition under way at the mission. He told Bringas:

> *they are now making two rooms in the old church adjacent to the church and house. It suits me greatly that one room is being built. Your Reverence already knows that there is only one room and it is very fitting that there should be two rooms where there are two Fathers. Thus each one may work without being disturbed by the other"* (Socies 1797).

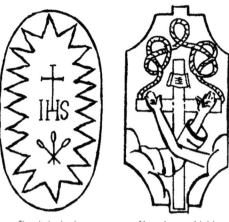

Jesuit insignia   *Franciscan shield*

In a salute to the first priests at San Xavier, the Franciscans depicted both their own insignia as well as that of the Jesuits on the façade, and retained Fr. Espinosa's baptismal font with the Jesuit monogram.

1967 looking south to the mortuary chapel: the two adobe rooms built in 1797 within Fr. Espinosa's 1757 church (Fr. Charles W. Polzer, S.J.).

Archaeology in 1967 at the site of Fr. Espinosa's church confirmed that the Franciscans built two rooms within its walls. Part of the east wall of the nave formed the east wall of the two adjacent rooms, while the remaining walls for the rooms were raised beneath the church's flat roof. The floors of the new rooms were tiled with fired brick left over from the construction of the church, then covered with lime plaster.

Perhaps taking Socies at his word about not enjoying the glories of San Xavier, his superiors in 1798 transferred him some 75 miles south-southeast to Mission Saric at the headwaters of the Río Altar (Dobyns 1976: 47).

The first detailed description of the finished church – finished, that is, except for the east tower and parts of the interior left partially decorated or undecorated – is that of Fr. Francisco Iturralde, the father president of the Pimería Alta missions, when he visited San Xavier on Sept. 23, 1797:

San Ygnacio de Loyola (1491-1556), founder of the Society of Jesus, in the prominent first niche to the right of the sanctuary – another example of Franciscan respect for the colleagues of San Xavier (Edward McCain).

Except for the pews, the tile floor, and some spotlights, San Xavier as seen here in November 2013 is virtually unchanged since 1797. At ease in the aisle is Princess, the now late but still much-admired dog owned by Jarvis Juan of Wa:k (William Steen).

I inspected the baptismal font, the Holy Oils, and the books of administration, and all is according to Roman ritual. ...

I visited the church and sacristy, which is a structure of two very good rooms whose construction is of burned brick and lime. The roof is barrel-vaulted. The church is very large. It has five altars, four in the transepts and the High Altar: the High Altar has a reredos of burned brick and lime, and it is painted and gilded, and the other altars are only painted, and all are adorned with 32 statues of saints including the four that are in the four pillars in the body of the church, and all are very beautiful. Moreover, the walls of the church, the octagonal drum, the high dome, as also the choir loft are adorned with various images and mysteries in fine paintings which are applied on the wall, but in such a manner that they appear to be on canvas. There are four windows in the drum of the crossing as well as four windows in the main body of the church, all with glass. The church has two towers, one unfinished, but the only thing lacking is the dome. The pavement of the floor of the church is of lime mortar and well-polished. In one of the towers is the baptistry with its good font and a door. It has plenty of room and is enclosed by walls of burned brick and lime and has a good door. It also has a new cemetery with walls of burned brick and lime and a door and a good chapel of the same material. All this structure is as new as today. It was started by the deceased Fr. Juan Bautista Velderrain, and for the greater part it was finished by Fr. Preacher Juan Bautista Llorens. It has barely the necessary vestments to celebrate the Holy Sacrifice of the Mass, which are already well-used, but they are well-kept as are also the sacred vessels (Iturralde 1797).

Iturralde also reported that the September 1797 population of Bac was 116 people: 35 married couples, six widowers and widows, and 40 unmarried people of both sexes and all ages (McCarty 1977a: 46).

On June 15, 1802, Fr. Llorens was joined by Fr. Ignacio José Ramírez y Arellano, a native of the province of Puebla east of Mexico City and a Franciscan since Dec. 11, 1798. Fr. Ramírez wrote a series of remarkable letters to his mother and brother. The letters were discovered, translated into English, and published by Fr. Maynard Geiger of Mission Santa Barbara, Calif. They tell a good deal about San Xavier from 1802 to 1805:

[to his brother:] *Get on a saddle some afternoon and come here for a ride and you will eat good watermelons and cantaloupes, peaches, grapes, pomegranates, and a thousand other things, for although we are poor, nothing is wanting to us. These things are ours because of good fortune and because of our labor, for in order to eat a fig from the fig tree, it is necessary to cover it with a protective awning because of the severe frosts which spare nothing. The pomegranates are exquisite. What we never lack during the greater part of the year are the melons and watermelons, especially the latter, which are very good ones.*

.... The snowfalls come every year and water is scarce, but not the storms which are many and terrible even though it does not rain. Now I am an everlasting exorcist for I have never anywhere seen the heavens so angry. What noises! What thunder! What wind! It appears that these elements wish to lift us and the house up to the stars .... Here one passes the time in a continual battle and struggle in all matters so that much patience is necessary, not the patience of nature, but of the patience we call virtue....

[to his mother:] *Our labors here are the same as those of a pastor anywhere, and to this is added the work of temporalities. This work of conquest is quite different from what it is considered to be down there. The neglect on the part of the government, if not the calculated disregard, to work for any advance here, stupefies us. A long time ago many people here could have become Christians without any difficulty and these even asked for priests. But those gentlemen on whom devolved the duty of supplying them looked only to their own personal interests and this matter of founding missions does not bother them. Though they do not offer any opposition, yet without their help, what can we do? Nothing! As a result, the only conquests we make are a few among those who are faced with hunger or threatened by enemies who come from their lands and even then some of them flee after they are Christians and thus everything is lost. It is a shame to see so many Yumas coming here from their territory every day and still no advantage is gained. The Indians are of such a disposition that only by force of arms are they conquered and subjected and by force of fear are they settled in towns. Even then only as a matter of routine do they accept Christianity.*

.... [The Apache Indians] are mortal enemies, not only of Christians, but of everybody. They go about the whole area robbing and killing to get what they can.... [T]hey have nothing else to do or nothing else to think of, nor are the many presidios which are located here for that reason only, of any avail to restrain them. For this reason the soldiers here are organizing a campaign against them .... not only the soldiers but the mission Indians in recent days, those of San Xavier and Tucsón which is a visita from here, together with Pápagos and Gileños, went out against them. Though these latter are pagans they realize that the Apaches are their enemies. They set out and accomplished something because they brought back seven alive, women and youths, and killed eight. However, the alcalde of the town was killed and four more were wounded (Geiger 1953: 8-9).

Fr. Ramírez died at San Xavier on Sept. 26, 1805, possibly of typhoid fever (Geiger 1953: 10-11). As his body lay in state, "the dead friar's face and tonsure glistened. They were moist. He was sweating. A healthy color had replaced the grayness of death, and 'a most sweet and delightful odor' seemed to come from his body. Yet he was plainly dead" (Kessell 19-6: 106).

Thinking they might be witnessing a miracle, the friars delayed his burial the next day. Word of what had happened reached Tucsón, and people from there hurried to the mission. But a few hours later, the sweating and sweet smell ceased and the padre was laid to rest, probably beneath the sanctuary (Kessell 1976: 206).

San Xavier was truly the wonder of the frontier. Writing on Aug. 4, 1804, Tucsón presidial commandant José Zúñiga responded to a questionnaire in which, among other things, he was asked about public works. His reply:

The only public work here that is truly worthy of this report is the church at San Xavier del Bac, ten miles from this presidio. Other missions here in the north should really be called chapels, but San Xavier is truly a church. It is 99 feet long. Its width is 22 feet in the nave and 60 feet at the transept that forms two side chapels.

The entire structure is of fired brick and mortar. The ceiling is a series of arches and domes. The interior is adorned with 38 full-figure statues, three "frame-figures" dressed in cloth garments, and innumerable angels and seraphim.

The façade is quite ornate, boasting two towers, one of which is unfinished. The atrium in front extends out 27½ feet. To the left of the atrium is a new cemetery surrounded by a fired brick- and lime-plastered wall measuring 82½ feet in circumference. At the far end of the cemetery is a domed chapel built of the same materials ....

Since soon after arriving in 1790, Fr. Llorens did his best to recruit to San Xavier and Tucsón the O'odham who lived to the north and west. These were the peoples called Pápagos by the Spaniards, and some of whom were later called Kohatk by students of Piman culture. The numbers of Bac's earlier inhabitants, the Sobaipuris of Fr. Kino's day and their direct descendants, had dwindled steadily due to devastating epidemics of Old World diseases such as smallpox (Dobyns 1976: 133-148, and Jackson 1994: 61-69).

The Spaniards at the Tucsón presidio since 1775 and the Indians already there took a dim view of outsiders competing for their land and scarce water, so the recruiting by Llorens was not always well received. He was often discouraged, too, when O'odham who moved to Tucsón and San Xavier would receive baptism but then leave and revert to their former ways.

In a report to Fr. Francisco Moyano on Dec. 27, 1811, Llorens said that in February 1794, residents of the northerly O'odham villages of Pipian and Santa Ana de Cuiquiburitac had agreed to recognize San Xavier as their mission with the latter village as a *visita*. The understanding was that after harvesting their crops at the end of October the northerners would move to Bac until April and receive Christian instruction. In 1810 and 1811, Llorens hauled timber from San Xavier to Cuiquiburitac to build a chapel, an adobe house, "and another small room that served to shelter the [military] escort and the few laborers with their families whom I had brought here during the past two years." Cuiquiburitac was near the southeastern base of Santa Rosa Mountain about half way between Tucsón and the Gila River. Thanks to Bac's pastor, Cuiquiburitac became Spain's "outpost of empire" in Sonora – the

La Purísima Concepción de Nuestra Señora de Caborca
San Xavier's slightly smaller-scale sister mission completed in May 1809 after six years of work under the same architect, Ygnacio Gauna (panoramio.com).

northernmost *visita* in the Pimería Alta under both Nueva España and México (Fontana 1987: 139-40).

In 1813, a Spaniard named Francisco Xavier Díaz, a cowboy employed by Fr. Llorens at San Xavier, murdered his wife, María Ignacia Castelo, in a fit of drunken jealousy. The immediate result was the first murder trial in Tucsón. From its records we know that the illiterate *mayordomo* of San Xavier was Venancio Salvatierra, born at the O'odham village of Aquituni (Ak Chin) on the lower Río Santa Cruz of an Indian and Spanish family. We also learn that a monolingual O'odham speaker named Eusebio was Bac's *alcalde* – its mayor. The outcome of the trial in 1814 (after lengthy legal review as typical of Spanish jurisprudence) was the execution of Díaz for the crime (McCarty 1976: 100-103).

Over his 25 years at Bac, Fr. Llorens continued to serve as pastor of San Xavier despite a growing disenchantment with his assignment. By 1814 he was assisted by Fr. Diego Gil (Dobyns 1976: 48). How long Gil had been at San Xavier and whether Llorens was helped by another priest after the death of Ramírez in 1805 is unknown but probable.

By 1797, Llorens had likely built the mud adobe walls around the graveyard – the *camposanto*. Over the next 18 years he arranged for the dismantling and re-use of what could be salvaged from Espinosa's old mud adobe church (Fontana 1973) and built three mostly mud adobe additions covering just over 5,400 square feet:

- The row or wing of rooms east of the east tower with an area almost identical to Espinosa's church at just over 2,500 square feet.

- An arcade with five arches to the west of the courtyard.

- Another arcade with six arches south of the courtyard and north of the east wing.

Renovations in the 1970s and early 1980s by contractor James Metz uncovered plaster *canales* or sluices extending to ground level on the east side of the east tower below its roof. Similar vestigial canales are still visible in the sacristy arcade beneath its mesquite and saguaro rib roof. So both the east wing and the sacristy arcade were built *after* work concluded on the new church in 1797.

East of the east tower the first room has five pine beams. One dates to no later than 1811 and is likely from the Rincon mountains (Herrick & Baisan 2019). As noted, Llorens in 1810 and 1811 hauled timber to Cuiquiburitac, but evidently saved some for this room at San Xavier and the next room with six similar beams. The two rooms would give Llorens and his assistant larger and nicer rooms closer to the church and the chapter room. And with their old rooms vacated, it allowed for dismantling of the first church.

The confirmation that most of that church survives in the east wing is seen in its two posts supporting mid-span lintels, and three of the four interior walls taking the place of the other posts. These posts and walls support over 65 feet of mid-span lintels and the half beams above them – the distinctive framing of Espinosa's roof.

In the sacristy arcade the five piers between the arches were built of smooth river rock dumped into lime mortar in rectangular excavations. At grade and for circa 40 inches up, the piers were built with irregular rock (possibly basalt) and leftover bits of fired brick.

The piers supported arches, upper walls, and a low parapet of mud adobe. Since the arcade helped shade the chapter room and the sacristy and because its lower piers required skilled masonry, the sacristy arcade is likely the first of the Llorens additions.

By 1814, Fr. Llorens had reached the limits of his patience. Some of the O'odham in Tucsón, apparently prodded by the non-Indians living there, had rebelled. Llorens placed part of the blame on Tucsón's presidial chaplain, Fr. Pedro Arriquibar, with whom he'd been quarreling at least since 1808 (Officer 1987: 93). All this was too much for Llorens. He asked his superiors to be transferred from Franciscans based at Querétaro to the Province of Jalisco. "I know," he wrote, "that it is impossible for me to stay on in peace at this mission of San Xavier and its *visita* of Tucsón." In 1815 he headed south, dying on the road at the presidio of Santa Cruz (Kessell 1976: 225, 239). Whether Fray Diego Gil was still at San Xavier is unknown.

The last of the first Franciscans: 1815-1843

In 1816, San Xavier got a new pastor. He was Mexican-born Fray Gregorio Ruiz. Originally from the Franciscan Province of Yucatán, he joined the Colegio de la Santa Cruz at Querétaro in December 1800, and was sent to the northern missions in 1802. Ruiz was at Tumacácori for most of 1807. His stay at San Xavier was short: he died there a violent death – just how is not stated – on Jan. 25, 1817 (Kessell 1976: 205 n. 63, 206, 239). San Xavier was again becoming the "unlucky mission of Bac" as during most of the Jesuit era, although in 1820 it was among the few Pimería Alta mission stations with more Indians than non-Indians listed in its census (Kessell 1976: 246).

San Xavier's next Franciscan missionary seems to have been Fr. Juan Vaño, a Spaniard born in Valencia who had come to Nueva España in 1813. He may have been at Bac earlier, but was definitely there by 1819. In the summer of 1821 he tried to buy the nearly 27 square miles of the Canoa Land Grant 35 miles to the south. On Sept. 27, México won its independence from Spain. He was still pastor at Easter 1824 (Dobyns 1960: 9; Kessell 1976: 247, 250-51, 257-58, 267).

Fr. Rafael Díaz succeeded Vaño that year. Born Oct. 24, 1794 just north of Cádiz in Spain, Díaz emigrated to Nueva España and entered the Franciscan Province of Michoacán in 1818 two days shy of his 24th birthday. In 1820 he transferred to the Querétaro college, and four years on was at a northern outpost (Kessell 1976: 277).

The Spanish birth of Díaz, Vaño, and other Quereteran friars destroyed most of their missionary careers in the Pimería Alta. In December 1827, the Mexican Congress expelled all Spaniards from México. The state governments were soon to follow suit, including that of the new Estado Occidente, the State of the West that now included the Pimería Alta. Even before that happened, however, the Spanish friars, accused of fomenting resistance to

their removal among their native charges, were ordered by the military in 1828 to vacate their missions. As the Jesuits had gone before them in 1767, now the Fransicscan sons of Spain were threatened with a similar fate. Fr. Díaz dutifully rode south, abandoning his church at San Xavier (Kessell 1976: 269-71).

It was not long before the Mexicans realized that without the Franciscans, many northern communities would have no priests. Occidente's governor invited some to stay, but only two of the Quereterans, Mexican-born José María Pérez Llera, whose health was failing, and Fr. Díaz, who had friends in Arizpe, accepted his offer (Kessell 1976: 274).

Pérez Llera and Díaz returned north in mid-July 1828 and both initially took up residence in San Ignacio, dividing the Pimería Alta between them. Díaz took charge of Cocóspera, Tumacácori, and his old mission of San Xavier. By the end of the year Díaz, now a naturalized Mexican, was living in Tucsón and presumably caring for San Xavier from there. The next year he was living in Cocóspera, but still responsible for churches in the Santa Cruz Valley. In 1832, when everyone in the region decided to wage a defensive war against the Apaches, Díaz invited to Cocóspera officials of nine "patriotic pueblos," including San Xavier, to form a militia (Kessell 1976: 277, 280, 284).

A drought in 1832 devastated crops. Fr. Díaz reported that most Indians at Tumacácori had no reserves of food and had been forced to leave their homes to work as laborers for settlers at starvation wages. He also complained that the soldiers at the presidios of Tucsón and Santa Cruz never responded when Apaches raided O'odham settlements. By 1834, he'd reached the end of his rope. He asked for a transfer to Nuevo México, but was refused. In response he settled in at Cocóspera from where he would ride circuit all the way to Tucsón (Kessell 1976: 288-89).

In the meantime, Fr. Pérez Llera had gone to Querétaro in 1833 to recruit more missionaries for the Pimería Alta. One of two priests who returned with him was Fr. Antonio González. Born in Salamanca in the central Mexican state of Guanajuato, González had become a Franciscan priest at the Querétaro college

Work on a larger church at Mission San José de Tumacácori 39 miles south of Bac began in 1800 but was suspended till 1821-1822 and never finished. This 1870 view shows the open-air ruins before reconstruction of the roof over the nave in 1919-1921 (Carlo Gentile, Library of Congress).

in February 1823. He was assigned to San Xavier, most likely in 1834 (Kessell 1976: 292, 296).

Fr. González had been at Bac for about two years when in April 1836, he wrote to the state governor complaining of outsider encroachments on O'odham and mission lands. One of the village Indians had killed a cow invading San Xavier fields, and González had been obligated to pay reparations. Besides that, the *alcaldes* were advising Indians that as citizens of México they no longer had to work for the mission. As a result, complained the friar, the Pápagos "do not want to do communal labor, as has always been the custom in the missions." Moreover, he said, if:

> … *your excellency does not take the measures that justice demands to end these damages that I am experiencing … I shall be forced to inform my prelate that I can no longer endure the discomfort stemming from these causes, and regretfully abandon these settlements and retire to my college to rest and recuperate* (Officer 1987: 138-39).

Thirty years later in 1866, Fr. Jean B. Salpointe found that strong elements of the Franciscan mission system, one applied without force of arms, survived at San Xavier. He interviewed men who had been employed by the priests as foremen in various jobs. They told him:

> … *the Indians were perfectly free to work for themselves or for the church, to cultivate their own fields or the church land, with the difference that the former had to look for their maintenance, while the latter were supported by the mission. Those who worked for the mission were dependent on it for food and clothing, not only for themselves but for their families. For that purpose provisions were stored in the mission house, or convent, and distributed in due time.*
>
> *Early in the morning the inhabitants of the pueblo had to go to church for morning prayers and to hear mass. Breakfast followed this exercise. Soon after, a peculiar bell called the workmen. They assembled in the atrium, a little place in front of and adjoining the church, where they were counted by one of the priests and assigned to the different places where work was to be done. … During the season of planting and harvesting, the workmen had dinner prepared for them in the farmhouse. Towards the evening a little before sundown, the work was stopped and the men permitted to go home. On their arrival in the houses which were located round the plaza, one of the priests, standing in the middle of this plaza, said the evening prayers in a loud voice in the language of the tribe. Every word he pronounced was repeated by some selected Indians who stood between him and the houses, and lastly by all the Indians present in the pueblo* (Salpointe 1898: 183-84).

González was San Xavier's last resident priest. Late in 1837 he transfered to Oquitoa in the Altar Valley. Fr. Díaz, then at San Ignacio, again became San Xavier's pastor in absentia, this time until his death in 1841. By then, says Kessell, "the remaining mission Indians wallowed in misery, vice, and ignorance of God, utterly insubordinate to their ministers. Mission property existed in name only, in 'hopeless disorder, for everything pertaining to the fields and lands is up for grabs to all.' Thus the economic base of the missionaries' spiritual ministry had crumbled" (Kessell 1976: 293).

Save for brief intervals over the next 36 years from 1837 to 1873, the villagers at Bac were the true custodians of the mission their forebears had built, and guardians of what remained of its sacred vessels (Fontana 1993b: 2).

San Xavier was unable to rely on the Tucsón soldiers for protection, so suffered considerably at the hands of Apaches and through general neglect with no priest. In October 1842, Pápagos at San Xavier became convinced that some of the so-called *manso* or peaceful Apaches living in Tucsón had run off San Xavier horses to turn over to their hostile relatives. The Pápagos tried to take matters into their own hands by attacking the Apaches in Tucsón even though they were under Mexican military protection. There was an altercation, no one was hurt, and the attackers from Bac apologized to the Mexican commandant the next day (Officer 1987: 160).

When Fr. Díaz died in 1841, González was still at Oquitoa, and nominally in charge of San Xavier. He left the Pimería Alta in mid-1842 but returned the following year to San Ignacio, this time as a member of the Franciscans' Jaliscan province rather than as a Quereteran. His mission territory was hopelessly large and he was able only occasionally to visit its many settlements, Bac included. In Feb. 7, 1843, he left the great church at San Xavier for the last time, riding there and to other Santa Cruz Valley stations with a military escort for protection against Apaches. When he died a short time later, the Spanish and Mexican era of the Franciscans at San Xavier died with him (Kessell 1976: 297, 302; Officer 1987: 162).

Diocese of Sonora and Sinaloa: 1844-1858

In late May 1843, Sonoran Sub-Prefect Joaquín Quiroga forwarded to state officials a May 11 report from the Tucsón justice of the peace, writing that at San Xavier:

> *Many of the burnt bricks are disintegrating, with the lime mortar washing out between them, all due to the sudden thunderstorms of summer and the long, continuing rains of winter. The moisture penetrates to the inside and is ruining the paintings. If this continues, due to the lack of repair since the religious went away* [in 1837], *the whole building will be reduced to a ruin within a very few years.*
>
> *The cemetery of the mission has its own chapel, also built of burnt brick. The chapel door is missing, but the doors of the church are all intact – each fitted with its own lock.*
>
> *The mission residence has 11 rooms, two of them of burnt brick, with all 11 facing an inside square, in turn graced with outer arches enclosing a covered corridor, also in ruin.*
>
> *Of the 11 rooms, four are roofed with massive crossbeams supported by heavy upright timbers. One or the other beam is broken, and as the saguaro ribs they support are rotting, the entire roof is coming down.*
>
> *A recreational garden of the religious* [north of the church, according to oral tradition], *surrounded by a wall that is falling down, boasted a variety of fruit trees, which, through lack of care, no longer bear fruit.*
>
> *The communal agricultural lands of the mission are no longer cultivated and lie barren. Only about an eighth part of these lands and of the garden are kept up by the native governor. The rest of the*

planting land is used by the natives of this village and those [about 40 families] of Santa Ana [de Cuiquiburitac], a remote village subject to the authority of the missionary at San Xavier. No non-Indians are involved. The majority of even the native residents are without sustenance and unable to farm. This is because of a recent lack of the necessary water, in turn due to neglect of keeping the river water moving and, instead, allowing it to gather in large stagnant pools along the sides.

San Xavier has no cattle and no sheep. The missionary himself [Fray Rafael Díaz] rounded them all up and either gave them away or sold them. He even took away the oxen, forcing the natives to plant with a stick or with borrowed oxen. Every year, a few of the mission's wild horses are broken in. These are divided up among the Indians in charge of keeping the fence mended. From within this fence the useless animals are turned loose. It was also from within this fence that the aforementioned missionary took possession of five mules for his own use with no benefit to the mission (McCarty 1997: 89-90).

Quiroga said the living quarters of the priests consisted of 11 rooms, a reference to the east wing he describes as close to ruin. This was, and remains today, the east-west wing next to the front of the church abutting its east bell tower. The collapsed galleries and fallen beams contrast with the comparatively good condition of the church, which was built of fired brick.

In 1844 the upkeep of Christian doctrine and practices at San Xavier became the responsibility of the Bishop of Sonora and Sinaloa, Dr. Lázaro de la Garza y Ballesteros, and fell into the hands of the very few circuit riding secular priests on the northern Sonoran frontier. Fr. Bachiller don Trinidad García Rojas, the secular priest then at the former mission of San Ignacio, visited the Santa Cruz Valley stations a couple of times a year from 1844 to 1848. In 1844 he performed three baptisms at San Xavier, then seven on Aug. 25 and 26, 1845, and eight on May 13, 1846. The baptismal records no longer indicated ethnicity, and since all the Pimas and Pápagos by then had Spanish names, it is impossible to know if those baptized were Indians or Mexicans. It is sure, though, that the numbers of Mexicans living at San Xavier was growing. In February 1847, García baptized 14 children at Bac, then 26 children just six months later (Almada 1983: 270-71; Kessell 1976: 302; Officer 1987: 188, 193, 203, 206).

Fr. García's visits came despite continued Apache raids throughout the region and, in December 1846, the passage through Tucsón of Lt. Col. Philip St. George Cooke and his Mormon Battalion. The party of 397 Mormon volunteers and career Army officers plus five wives was on its way from recently captured Santa Fé to engage Mexican forces in California. As Cooke's force neared Tucsón on Dec. 17, the some 100 Mexican troops at the presidio under Antonio Comadurán withdrew to San Xavier. Cooke's brief stay in Tucsón was peaceful, and although he set out toward Bac to confiscate arms and other supplies, the battalion encountered heavy mesquite in which it feared ambush, so returned to Tucsón, then continued west (Officer 1987: 194-201; Sheridan 1986: 24).

The Mormon Battalion had approached Tucsón from the southeast between the Rincon and Santa Rita mountains. On Dec. 16, 1846, Cooke wrote in his diary:

We saw, as we marched over the plains, far to the left [southwest], a very large stone church built by the Jesuits [sic]; it is at a large Indian Pueblo, about ten miles above …. There are several Pueblos in the close vicinity" (Cooke 1848: 42).

P. S. G. Cooke (dragooned.blogspot.com).

Today it seems ironic that by far the largest and most elaborate of Spanish colonial structures within hundreds of miles was within sight but never approached or entered by the first known English-speaker to mention it in print.

Pinaleño Apaches regularly attacked both Tubac and San Xavier in the 1840s. Shortly after a visit by Fr. García to San Xavier and Tucsón from Aug. 28 to Sept. 1, 1847, 45 troops from the presidio plus 32 from Tubac and Santa Cruz and 133 Pima and peaceful Apache auxiliaries rode out on a successful punitive expedition. Four days later, the Pimas, some no doubt from San Xavier, were among the attackers at Aravaipa Canyon 50 miles north-northeast. The outnumbered Apaches were soundly beaten, 16 warriors, 7 women, and 4 boys killed, and 14 Pinaleños captured (Officer 1987: 206-07).

In late December 1847 and January 1848, Bachiller Lorenzo Vázquez of Altar, another secular priest, made the rounds in the Santa Cruz Valley on behalf of Vicar Forane Francisco Javier Vásquez. He "was completing one of the most exhausting religious

October 1848: the first known depiction of San Xavier (Chamberlain 1956).

Oct. 9, 1849: Mission San Xavier and Bac drawn by H.M.T. Powell (1931: facing 144).

xpeditions since the days of Garcés. He had traveled nearly 200 miles before he reached [Tucsón] in late December. Facing him at Tucsón and San Xavier was a large accumulation of sacramental responsibilities" (Officer 1987: 220). While at Bac he baptized 21 people, confirmed 76, and confessed 22. By Jan. 16 he was back at his home base (Kessell 1976: 310).

On May 28, 1848, the Treaty of Guadalupe Hidalgo ended the two-year war between México and the United States. México lost nearly half its territory, but Sonora kept a comparatively small swath of land lying mostly south of the Gila River – the area that today s Southern Arizona. Tucsón and San Xavier remained in Sonora.

In October, U.S. dragoons commanded by Maj. Lawrence P. Graham passed by San Xavier on their way from Monterey in Nuevo León to California. One of the soldiers, Samuel Chamberlain, painted the earliest known view of San Xavier, including the ving east of the church (Chamberlain 1956: 77).

Another of Graham's soldiers, Lt. Cave Johnson Couts, provided what is apparently the earliest Anglo-American written account of the mission's appearance:

The Church at <u>Xavier del Bac</u>, which we left this morning, is said to be the <u>finest</u> in Sonora. 'Tis truly a noble and stupendous building. Its domes and spires which projected above the thick mesquite growth as we approached was of itself sufficient to guarantee a City with <u>many</u> churches and other large and fine buildings. But when we came up, found it standing solitary and alone, not another building nearer to it than <u>Tucson</u>, save the few old Indian huts of the most rude description, whose inmates (Pimas) had charge of the fine old church. It is built of <u>burnt brick</u>, the first any of us had seen in Mex. and was built by the Spaniards as an Indian Missionary. The dressing, which always attends their churches, is truly magnificent. Wax figures [sic] and paintings, particularly fine. Standing under the large dome and looking directly up, its whole inner surface is a complete elegant painting, indeed

the same might be said of its <u>whole interior surface</u>, oil [sic] paintings. The faces are all exceedingly handsome. The Wax [sic] figure of the Virgin Mary, deprived of one arm [?] by <u>time</u> has as handsome a face as I ever saw. The exterior shows no age: on the contrary looks rather new: but there is an appearance of age about the interior which rather adds to than deteriorates from the sublimity of the picture. It is kept by these Pimas with incredible care and neatness (Couts 1961: 61-62).

The occasional Mexican military success notwithstanding, in 1848 Apaches forced the abandonment of most of the settlements in the Santa Cruz Valley. Tucsón and Bac remained as armed sanctuaries, but in December, Apaches all but destroyed Tubac. That was too much for those still living there as well as for the Pimas in neighboring Tumacácori. Historian John L. Kessell says the 25 to

30 Pimas "took down the Santos from their niches in the church, bundled up vestments and sacred vessels, and followed the retreating settlers [from Tubac] down the road to San Xavier. To add to their suffering that winter, it was colder than any of them could remember and snow blew across the desert. Come spring they hoped to return" (Kessell 1976: 308).

Encarnación Mamake, the elderly San Xavier Sobaipuri who some 80 years later told Fr. Bonaventure Oblasser about her family's tradition about the "Mexican" who decorated the interior of San Xavier, had a personal recollection of the arrival at Bac:

San Cayetano (1480-1547): charred by Apaches in 1848 (Vern Lamplot).

Tumacácori belongs to us, too. It happened this way. The Apaches drove out our kin folks from that mission. These wild people were going to burn the statue of San Cayetano. The flames had already commenced to consume the image, when a shower extinguished the fire. This statue and many others were brought here by the women, who carried them in their kiahats [burden baskets]. The statue of María Santísima, however, was brought tied on a horse. I missed seeing the cavalcade arrive at the old mission, but I did hear the ringing of the mission bells as they reached this place. One of the statues, the one of the Blessed Virgin with child, was taken to Tucsón (Oblasser 1930-31: 98).

The Tumacácori Pimas were absorbed by their fellow O'odham at Bac and Tucsón, their old mission fell into ruin, and the sacred treasures they had carried to San Xavier stayed there until 1973 in the case of five statues and till 2007 for a sixth statue. Statues returned in 1973 to what was then Tumacácori National Monument (now Tumacácori National Historical Park) were those of saints Cayetano, Francisco de Asís, Buenaventura, Pedro de Alcántara, and Antonio de Padua with the Christ Child. A processional figure of Jésus Nazareno was returned to Tumacácori in 2007. Still at San Xavier – and likely to remain – are the statues of San Xavier reclining, San José, and the La Inmaculada at the north altar in the east transept (Ahlborn 1974: 80-81, 103, 111-115).

The discovery of gold in California on Jan. 24, 1848 led to the great overland rush of 1849. One of several major trails to the western land of dreams took countless gold seekers through Sonora and the village of Bac. Many left their names scrawled on the walls of the church, a few of which can still be seen. A handful of the argonauts left their names on diaries, letters, and reminiscences that have survived the passage of time (Aldrich 1950: 49-52; Beeching 1849: 23; Clarke 1852: 85-86; Cox 1925: 142-43; Durivage 1937: 210; Eccleston 1950: 198-201; Evans 1945: 150-51; Hunter 1992: 152-56; Murichson and Birt 1966; Pancoast 1930: 234-35; Powell 1931: 145; Wood 1955).

Fortunately for posterity, a talented artist in the person of H.M.T. Powell paused long enough at San Xavier on Oct. 9, 1849 to make one of the best pencil drawings of the early church and surrounding village. His impression: "It is, with the exception of the Church, a most miserable hole." He wrote in his diary that the church's roof leaked and predicted that in a few years it would fall into total ruin (Powell 1931: facing 144, 145). Another '49er, Robert Eccleston, also drew the mission, but his drawing hasn't survived (Eccleston 1950: 199).

Baltimore-born Benjamin Hayes, later a pioneer Los Angeles county attorney and judge, visited San Xavier in 1849. His description, written Dec.13, exemplifies those by other '49ers and early Anglo-Americans:

This morning early went up to the village. Struck with the strange appearance of Indian wigwams on one side, and adobes on the other; still more with the splendid church of solid structure, whose dome and belfries overlook the town and a wide extent of mountain and plain. Staid there until 10 o'clock when finally succeeded in getting sight of the interior. Our first visit was to the church – the splendor of the outside and a glimpse of the beauty through a high window, exciting our curiosity to the highest. We asked a Mexican to admit us. He told us a Pimo had the key, pointing to the wigwam. On going there, he sent us to another Pimo. Finally, for a while, we abandoned the attempt, and I traded percussion caps for beans. Fired revolver, which seemed to please

them, I mean, the Indians. A Pimo sent for a pistol; it would not stand cocked. Fired it for him, and then an old double-barreled shot gun, nearly as bad to cock. At length a Pimo spoke in his language across the plaza to have us admitted, [and] in Spanish, to send two of the muheres [mujeres] with us. They kept us waiting half an hour, meantime I examined the other premises. The delay itself seemed to have been made only to astonish & please us, the more.

Two belfries, hexagonal base, the octagonal on it, then smaller dome-shapes with cross on top of the whole, whole height of belfry finished perhaps 160 feet [sic]. Two bells in completed belfry, one of the other belfry which seems never to have been completed. Dome back of the belfries, over the altar. Terrace on top of the hole very pretty. Beautiful front, with niches for figures, some of them now defaced a good deal. High wall on the east, enclosing rooms with lofty ceilings, which may once have been a monastery; staircase view from interior gallery, and two galleries outside; floors solid cement, in square blocks. 3 altars. Light and airy appearance of ceiling over altar, with white, pink, and blue colors. Statues innumerable of saints, Apostles, Blessed Virgin, etc. 12 oil paintings by masters, sent no doubt from Europe; appear to be old, and to a connoisseur would be of great value. Besides, numerous fine paintings on the walls, some very large, of Scriptural scenes, and the colors fresh as if painted yesterday. Four old missals in a closet in the sacristy, which the girls, thinking doubtless that we would be interested in their treasures, unlocked for us. Oldest printed in 1762, another in 1769. Parish records of births, etc. Oldest date in latter 1765. No seats. Side rooms, sacristy, etc., all highly finished. Splendid cornice. Gilded carved pilasters, making the altar, in the light of the sun's rays straying through a lofty window, glitter like a mass of gold. Girls showed us "San Antonio Chiquito," a very pretty little figure, on which she put a neat little cap of pink silk, and laughed at its beauty. The bier with a coffin. The Padre is to be here in three days. I was told by a Mexican that the church was built 200 years ago; a Pimo dissented, saying 'más'….

July 19, 1852: a drawing by Henry C. Pratt (Hall: 1996).

El Santo: Carried from Tumacácori north to San Xavier in December 1848 by Pimas retreating from the Apaches

San Xavier reclining in his bier in the west transept – the focus of thousands of pilgrims and other worshipers since 1849. The petitioners pray for the Santo to intercede for them or for loved ones, especially those seeking cures for ills of all sorts. Photos, hospital wrist bands, and milagros (small metal depictions of hearts, lungs, or whatever area in distress) are pinned to San Xavier's blanket in acts of petition or of thanks, and votive candles lit nearby (Edward McCain).

San José left, and, at right, La Inmaculada, both originally at Tumacácori till December 1848 (Edward McCain).

Besides San Cayetano, the four Santos returned to Tumacácori in 1973 after 125 years at San Xavier (Vern Lamplot)

San Francisco de Asís
ca. 1181-1286

San Buenaventura
1221-1274

San Pedro de Alcántara
1499-1562

San Antonio with El Niño
1195-1231

Jésus Nazareño returned in 2007 after 159 years

The sotocoro Cristo at the entry

El Nazareño in 2002 in San Xavier's baptistery (Edward McCain).

Some estimate that the crucifix at the entry dates to the last half of the 1800s and was likely made in Mexico (Ahlborn 1974: 107).
But 1840s inventories of Tumacácori list a crucifix, as does an 1855 account of items at San Xavier belonging to Tumacácori (Giffords 1978: 89, 95, 99, 103) (Edward McCain).

Their land around the village produces, they say, fine corn, wheat & beans, one fine garden. No fruit that I saw. The sepulchre of the church. Day very pleasant. They say it is a good year – little snow, but that they sometimes have much snow. A rocky hill just by the village had a cross on it, probably a cemetery, as the old one must be filled up. In the latter, a cross in the niches and over one or two of the graves. … A small and neat [mortuary] chapel – cement floor – cross over earth on one side of it – concave ceiling gives a pleasant echo. Some Apaches in hay wigwams, it is said. 7½ miles to Tucson (Hayes 1929: 43-45).

Waves of emigrants followed close on the heels of the '49ers to what they hoped would be the pot of gold beneath the rainbow of California. William P. Huff was at San Xavier on April 18, 1850. Nearly a quarter century later he penned his reminiscences of his overland journey, a recollection apparently aided by notes or with letters written at the time. His extremely detailed description of the mission contains obvious errors, but corroborates much of what Hayes and other wrote on the spot (Hosmer and others 1991: 50-53).

In February, a group of Tucsonans had petitioned for a priest. They said the Papagos had been especially neglected. It had been over a year since Fr. Vázquez returned to Altar.

The pueblo of San Xavier del Bac, of catechized Indians, is composed of more than 50 families. Because they have no pastor to propagate the Faith they live practically as heathens. Because it is a cabecera [head mission] close to the tribes of the west and the Gila who annually come in to this pueblo, many desire the water of baptism. And because it has no priest they are not being catechized. Even the natives of this pueblo and its visita of Tucsón have gone back to heathenism. This is the result of their having no shepherd of the flock of Jesus Christ (Kessell 1976: 310-11).

Bishop Garza in Culiacán nearly 1,100 miles south had no one he could send, and in September left to become archbishop of México. In 1851, however, Bernardino Pacheco, the parish priest of Santa Cruz (the Soamca of Fr. Kino's day), visited Tucsón and probably Bac (Officer 1987: 60-61).

Tucsón officials found themselves responsible for accommodating the settlers from Tubac whom Apaches had forced from their homes in late 1848. One of the refugees was José María Martínez, and early in 1851 he sought land near San Xavier. This required the cooperation of the Bac O'odham, whose governor was José Golosa, the adopted son of former village governor Ignacio Zapata. Matters were worked out between the parties, and on Feb. 24, 1851, Martínez was given a grant of land east of San Xavier. His descendants remained there until the early 1900s (Officer 1987: 253-54), and some are buried in front of the mortuary chapel.

In 1852, John R. Bartlett led the U. S. Boundary Commission in working with Mexican counterparts to survey the 1848 border. Bartlett was a literary man uniquely unqualified for the job and who spent much time exploring far afield on both sides of what was supposed to be the new border. He visited San Xavier on July 19. "This church," he wrote, "has more pretensions to architectural beauty than any I saw in the country" (Bartlett 1854: II: 298). Henry Cheever Pratt, one of the commission's illustrators, sketched the mission in pencil and later converted it to a watercolor with enhanced landscape (Hine 1968: Plate 40). One of Bartlett's surveyors, Andrew B. Gray, saw the church on Sept. 24, 1851, describing it in detail (Gray 1852: 267-68).

Though Mexican rule would continue till March 1856, San Xavier and Tucsón officially became part of the United States on June 30, 1854 after ratification of the $10 million Gadsden Purchase. Payment of $337 per square mile (about $9,500 in today's dollars) bought nearly 30,000 square miles and the real prize as seen at the time – an all-year route for a railway to the Pacific. Gone was the 1848 border along the Gila River to just west of today's Thatcher, south almost to modern Willcox, then east to the Rio Grande. Like lands north of the 1848 border, the new land became part of the Territory of New Mexico until the creation of the Arizona Territory in 1863.

Within weeks after the Gadsden Purchase, German tourist Julius Froebel visited San Xavier in July 1854. "I can scarcely recall any surprise greater," he wrote, "than I experienced at the sight of the buildings of the old and celebrated mission of San Xavier del Bac, standing in a region of sublime and simple grandeur." His taste for the baroque, however, was tempered. In the church's interior he found, "by the side of tasteless carvings and barbarous decorations ... an altar richly overlaid with gold [leaf]." Still, he was sufficiently impressed that he used a somewhat fanciful engraving of the mission complex as the frontispiece for his travel book (Froebel 1859: frontispiece, 499).

Circa Feb. 22, 1855: a lithograph in the Parke rail site survey (Library of Congress).

The Gadsden Purchase necessitated a new border survey. This time the American in charge was the highly qualified W. H. Emory of the Corps of Topographical Engineers. On June 29, 1855, near where Nogales would be founded 25 years later, Emory met with seven Gila River Pimas and two captains from San Xavier: Head Chief José Victoriano Lucas and Chief José Antonio. The commissioner:

informed them that by the terms of the treaty, all the rights that they possessed under Mexico are guaranteed to them by the United States; a title to lands that was good under the Mexican government is good under the U.S. government .... (Emory 1857: 96)

The Papagos had heard the first of many Anglo-American promises to follow (Fontana 1976: 111).

Emory's surveyor, Nathaniel Michler, described 1855 San Xavier as:

A beautiful church, with its exterior walls richly ornamented, carved, and stuccoed, and the interior handsomely decorated and painted in bright colors, with many fine paintings in fresco, still stands as a monument to the zealous labor and religious enthusiasm of the Jesuits [sic] *in the last century* (Michler 1857: 118).

The West was expanding rapidly. After the survey a series of explorers searched for the best route for the railroad. Lt. John G. Parke, whose job was to survey a portion of the route along the 32nd parallel near today's Pima Mine Road, barely missed the mission on Feb. 22, 1855, but that someone saw it is attested to by the lithograph of the church appearing in the report (Parke 1857: facing p. 35).

Historian Jim Officer says that before departing with local troops in May 1855, Ensign Joaquín Comadurán "inventoried all the furnishings at the Tucsón, San Xavier, and Tumacácori churches and forwarded a copy to his assistant inspector general. He then locked the … [churches]. José María Martínez was given the keys to … San Xavier and Tumacácori …. His orders were to open them only when priests visited and to put everything back in its proper place when they left." In March 1856 the last Mexican troops left Tucsón, heading south to Ímuris about 45 miles beyond the new border. Tucsón became Tucson (Officer 1987: 281).

In 1858 Phocian R. Way of Ohio arrived at San Xavier, noting in his diary for June 16 that:

The birds are its only occupants and they sing praises from morning until night. They build their nests on the heads of the saints and warble their notes of joy while perched on their fingers. They do not respect the sacred image of Christ, for a noisy swallow has built her nest in the crown of thorns that circles his brow, and at this moment is perched on his bleeding hand scolding loudly at my near approach. The door is always left open, but the property of the church is not disturbed. The natives look upon the structure with a feeling of awe and could not be persuaded to deface or injure it. If this country should ever again become thickly populated, it will be renovated and repaired and again used as a place of worship (Duffen 1960: 164).

Phocian Way was a prophet.

Diocese of Santa Fe: 1858-1866

Within a few weeks in St. Louis, the Catholic Church took notice of the new configurations of the United States and Mexico. Delegates to the Second Provincial Council that opened in mid-summer discussed adding the Gadsden Purchase to the Santa Fe Diocese under

Bishop Jean Baptiste Lamy. Most of the region had remained under the jurisdiction of the Bishop of Sonora and Sinaloa, who in 1858 was Pedro Loza y Pardavé. Tucson and San Xavier, if visited by a Mexican priest at all that year, was most probably served by the parish priest at Magdalena, J.M. Pineiro (Almada 1983: 384-85; Bell 1932: 315; Martínez and Anonymous 1858).

What the delegates to the Council did not know initially was that Rome had decreed on June 10 that the county of "Doñana" and the parish of Las Cruces be placed under jurisdiction of the Bishop of Santa Fe. The United States regarded the Gadsden Purchase as a westward extension of New Mexico's Doña Ana County (Horgan 1975: 257, 259, 261).

As soon as he learned of Rome's approval, Bishop Lamy relieved his vicar general of that post because he had an important new assignment for him. He was Fr. Joseph Projectus Machebeuf, born Aug. 11, 1812, in Riom in the Province of Auvergne in France. Fr. Machebeuf's job was to obtain the necessary concurrence from Bishop Loza for the takeover. He left Santa Fe on Nov. 3, 1858 (Horgan 1975: 261; Howlett 1908: 21).

In early January 1859, Machebeuf "… came to the Indian village of St. Francis Xavier among the Pima Indians, a tribe almost all Catholics. I had the pleasure of finding there a large brick church, very rich and beautiful for that country" (Howlett 1908: 246).

The priest continued south-southeast over 370 miles, finding the Sonoran bishop at a house north of Alamos where on Jan. 16, 1859, Loza readily relinquished jurisdiction of Tucson, San Xavier, and Tubac (Horgan 1975: 263-68).

Machebeuf, the future bishop of Denver, loved San Xavier because he had there not only a good church, but faithful villagers. His fellow pioneer Jean B. Salpointe, after retiring as Archbishop of Santa Fe, recalled that Machebeuf at San Xavier:

…. had only to send somebody to ring the bells to have all the people in church for Mass. These Indians had not forgotten the prayers they had been taught by the Franciscan Fathers, and they were ready to say them rather in Spanish than in their own language. Some of them could sing at Mass in a very tolerable manner, which is practiced yet [1898] *by some Mexicans who lived in the pueblo and learned it from the Indians. When the Vicar General made his first visit to San Xavier, he was agreeably surprised when the governor or chief of the tribes, José [Antonio Morales], told him that he had kept in his house, since the expulsion of the Franciscan Fathers, the sacred vessels, for fear that they might be stolen if they had been left in the church. The objects saved were: four silver chalices, a gold plated silver monstrance, two gold cruets with a silver plate, two small silver candlesticks, two silver censers and a sanctuary carpet* (Salpointe 1898: 227).

On his return to Santa Fe, Fr. Machebeuf prepared a report of his trip to the Gadsden Purchase and Sonora and sent it to the Society of the Propagation of the Faith. On May 3, 1859 he headed back, reaching Tucson in June, and staying in the area until September. "He also took steps for the repair and preservation of the old Mission Church of San Xavier del Bac. This old church … was a ruin like the rest of the Mission churches, but it was susceptible of repair and partial restoration. At subsequent visits he urged the further work and succeeded in putting it in such condition that it could be used for services" (Howlett 1908: 251).

January 1864 painting by John Ross Browne: Villagers celebrate the return of Fr. Aloysius Bosco with a new Jesuit, Fr. C.E. Messea.

If the Roman Catholic Church was beginning to bestir itself in Southern Arizona, so was the U.S. Dept of Indian Affairs. As early as 1857, Col. John Walker had been appointed agent for the Pimas and Papagos in the Gadsden Purchase. He resigned in 1858, then resumed his duties in 1859 and 1860. Walker headquartered in Tucson but San Xavier's Papagos – today's Tohono O'odham – were among his primary concerns till the Tennessean left to join the Confederate cause. There was no agent in 1861, but Abraham Lyon filled the post in 1862-63 (Fontana 1976: 115-125).

Bishop Lamy had his difficulties in getting priests for Tucson and San Xavier. From Oct. 15 to 19, 1861, a Padre Berdugo baptized 54 in Tucson, and in 1862 a Padre Serrano baptized another 46 people there from Aug. 28 to Sept. 3. In the same year a wandering Italian-born ex-Franciscan named Donato Rogieri (or "Rogerio" as he signed his name in the Las Cruces registers; or "Rogier" in the Tucson baptismal book) arrived and began construction on a future cathedral, San Agustín. The mud adobe walls were going up in November 1863 when he left to return to New Mexico. There is no evidence that Rogieri ever carried out any clerical duties at San Xavier, and just 10 baptisms are credited to him in Tucson (San Agustín Cathedral 1863-1878: Nov. 13, 1863; Salpointe 1898: 240; Sonnichsen 1982: 67).

A Jesuit, Fr. Aloysius Luis María Bosco, performed his first three baptisms at San Xavier on April 25, 1863. Born in Italy in 1815, Fr. Bosco joined the Society of Jesus in Turin in 1833, was ordained in 1844, and arrived in California in 1856. At Santa Clara College he taught Spanish until 1859. With encouragement from his Santa

Clara superior, Fr. Burcardo Villiger, Fr. Bosco wrote to Bishop Lamy in 1862, asking permission to go to the Gadsden Purchase where "there is hope of establishing a permanent Mission at San Xavier del Bac" (Anonymous n.d.a; Bosco 1862; San Agustín Cathedral 1863-1878: April 25, 1863. See Fox 1974 for an excellent discussion of the formative years of the Vicariate Apostolic of Arizona).

In December 1863, Fr. Bosco returned to California to meet Fr. Carolus Evasius Messea, a fellow Jesuit assigned to join him in Arizona. Messea, like Bosco, was born in Italy in 1815. They arrived in Yuma around Christmas, and traveled to Tucson in the company of newly appointed Arizona Supt. of Indian Affairs Charles D. Poston, U.S. Treasury agent and journalist John Ross Browne, and an escort from Company G, 1st Cavalry commanded by Capt. Samuel A. Gorham. Browne wrote that "The reverend fathers entertained us during our sojourn with an enthusiastic account of their plans for the restoration of the mission and the instruction and advancement of the Indian tribes…" (Anonymous n.d.b; Browne 1974: 142; Poston 1865).

In January 1864, Bosco took over at San Agustín, where he would perform 113 baptisms versus only a half dozen at San Xavier. Messea took up duties at the mission. Poston, who apparently did not realize that Bosco would work chiefly in Tucson, described the priests' arrival at Bac:

… It was a strange coincidence, that two Jesuit fathers, from the Santa Clara College in California, accompanied us to their long neglected neophytes. They were received by the Indians with great demonstrations of joy; and amid the ringing of bells and explosion of

Earliest known photo of San Xavier: circa 1867 by William A. Bell, surveyor for the Kansas Pacific Railway (Arizona State Archives).

fire-works, entered into possession of the long-neglected mission of San Xavier. These pious fathers immediately commenced laboring, with the zeal and fidelity of their order, and in a few days had the mass regularly chanted by the Papagos maidens with the peculiar softness of their language. Every facility was rendered the holy fathers in holding intercourse with the Indians, and a great improvement was soon perceptible in their deportment and habits. They seemed entering on a new era of moral and material prosperity, refreshing to witness, arising from these ruins (Poston 1865: 297-98).

Fr. Messea's account of his arrival at San Xavier confirms Poston's description:

... Both the Protestant and Catholic Indians have shown themselves to be well pleased at the arrival of the Fathers. As soon as the Indians called Papagos saw us coming, they ran to the Church towers and began ringing the seven bells as though the village were on fire. We went to the Church and gave thanks to God and recited the Rosary with the Indians. The next day we sang the Te Deum and gave the benediction. A good number of Indians come to Mass every day and sing songs in Spanish. ... These Indians are good, hardworking, and docile, and they treat us with courtesy. If the Bishop gives us Tucson, two Fathers and a Brother can live here very well (Messea, quoted in Villiger 1864).

Messea said the floor of the church "is a kind of Venetian pavement," and knew that fellow Jesuits had served the church until the 1767 expulsion. The last at San Xavier:

.... as appears from the Baptismal Register, was Fr. Ignacio Espinola [sic; Alonso Espinosa]. The convent, or house is in ruins. All the damage to the Church and the House was done not by Indians but by whites during the war between the Americans and the Mexicans. In former times the Church was exceedingly rich; now all that is left are two silver candelabra, two pyx, three chalices, and a few other trifles (Messea, in Villiger 1864).

Journalist Browne (1974: 143) drew a picture of the Jesuits' arrival at San Xavier for posterity, noting in the caption of his original sketch

that the occasion also marked the arrival of Col. M. Oliver Davidson, the Indian agent for the Papagos appointed by Supt. Poston. Davidson, however, seems to have been more interested in mining than in Indians, moving his headquarters to the Enriqueta Mines near Arivaca in 1864-65.

Fr. Messea immediately went to work to start a school at the mission. His efforts were recognized by the first governor of the new Territory of Arizona, John N. Goodwin, as well as by the Joint Committee on Education which on Oct. 27, 1864 observed: "At the Mission of San Xavier del Bac, Padre Messaya [sic], has at great trouble and expense to himself, educated all children free of charge. His pupils are Mexican and Papago. He has been sadly impeded in his efforts by want of suitable school books" (Anonymous n.d.b).

Bishop Lamy had visited San Agustín in March 1864, entering his name in the church's baptismal register on Easter, March 27. Fr. Bosco remained in Southern Arizona till at least Aug. 8, 1864, but when he and Fr. Messea departed, the bishop had no one he could spare. Tucson and San Xavier passed 17 more months without benefit of clergy.

The First Legislative Assembly of Arizona passed an "Act to Appropriate Money for the Aid of Public Schools" on Nov. 7, 1864. Section 1 appropriated $250 for the "Mission School of and at San Xavier del Bac, for the purpose of purchasing books of instruction...." But what would have been the first school in Arizona funded with public monies never opened. Messea and Bosco were gone but not forgotten according to Salpointe (241: 1898):

The people have kept up a good remembrance of their stay among them; the San Xavier Indians especially were formerly fond of speaking of Father Mesea [sic], as a man who pleaded their cause with the agent, to get from him the agricultural implements they needed, besides caring zealously for their spiritual welfare.

Second photo circa 1867: late afternoon from the southwest with all 10 estípite columns on the façade in place (Arizona State Archives).

J. B. Salpointe's
Tucson Vicariate: 1866-1885

Finally on Jan. 6, 1866, three priests, Jean Baptiste Salpointe, Francis Boucard, and Patrick Birmingham, plus a "Mr. Vincent," an "ecclesiastical student," left Santa Fe on the dangerous journey through Apache terrain to Tucson, arriving on Feb. 7. Fr. Salpointe, as vicar general, was stationed in Tucson with Boucard as his assistant. Birmingham went on to Yuma. Vincent was soon sent to re-open the school at San Xavier for the Papagos, but it "lasted only a few months, owing to the carelessness of the Indians in regards to the education of their children. The teacher was then removed to Tucson, where there appeared better prospects for a good school" (Salpointe 1898: 242, 252-53). Salpointe neglects to mention that the U.S. government would not hire Vincent as a teacher for Papagos because, as their Indian agent observed, he "could not speak a word of English" (Fontana 1976: 124).

Despite this setback, the ecclesiastical future of the mission was assured. Secular clergy permanently stationed in Tucson began frequent trips to the mission to perform weddings and baptisms, celebrate Mass, and bury the dead. On Sept. 25, 1868, the

Territory of Arizona was made a Vicariate Apostolic independent of Santa Fe with Salpointe as its Bishop-elect (technically, its Vicar Apostolic). Salpointe went to his native France where he was formally consecrated on June 20, 1869, then to Rome to meet Pope Pius IX (Fox 1974: 260; Salpointe 1898: 259-60).

Meanwhile, Davidson had resigned as Indian agent on April 20, 1866. Dr. Charles H. Lord, a contract surgeon at the Cerro Colorado mine near Arivaca, served as sub-agent for part of the year, but Davidson successor Levi Ruggles from 1866 to 1869 worked 90 miles to the northwest from the Gila River Indian Reservation created for the Pimas and Maricopas. So did his 1870 replacement, Frederick E. Grossman (Fontana 1976: 115-125; Sonnichsen 1982: 92-93).

Salpointe's first years in Southern Arizona were marked by a devastating epidemic of what he said was later called the "shaking fever," but which Indian Agent F.E. Grossman labeled as smallpox (Fontana 1976: 125). The vicar apostolic believed it had been

> *brought into Arizona in 1866 by the coming from Sonora of many poor people who fled from their country on account of the war after the intervention of France. The places that suffered most from this fever were Tucson, San Xavier, Tubac and the San Pedro settlements. From 1869 the plague abated sensibly, so that in 1870 there were only some scattered cases of it (Salpointe 1898: 256).*

Some 60 years later, the elderly San Xavier Sobaipuri, Encarnación Mamake, was probably recalling this epidemic when she told Fr. Bonaventure Oblasser (1930-31: 98):

*Carlo Gentile 1868 or 1870: the first known interior photo of San Xavier.
No chairs and no pews, and the original floor of lime plaster
(Library of Congress).*

A National Scandal: the Camp Grant Massacre

In late April 1871, after Apaches stole 19 cattle and horses near Bac and other attacks in Southern Arizona, San Xavier Chief Francisco Galerita agreed to join Tucsonans in a counter raid. The chief led 91 Papagos, including about 20 on horseback and some from Pan Tak below Kitt Peak. They met 48 Hispanics and six Anglos, crossed today's Redington Pass, headed north along the San Pedro, and before dawn on April 30 attacked the Apaches at Aravaipa Creek, clubbing, knifing, and then shooting 100 or more, mostly women and children. At least 27 children were captured by the San Xavier Papagos. Some were said to have been sold into bondage in Sonora, and R.A. Wilbur, the Indian agent, reported six in the homes of Leopoldo Carrillo and other Tucson Hispanics. Over 70 Papagos and over 20 Hispanics and Anglos were indicted for murder: 99 or 100 in total. At a December trial the jury returned after 19 minutes, finding all the accused not guilty (Officer 1987: 308, 403; Schellie 1968: 107, 116-118, 125, 242-247).

Something that brought great sadness to my people was an awful epidemic, many years ago. Most of my kin folks died from it. That is why but two of us are left of the old [Sobaipuri] people. All the rest here are Papagos, who have come from the desert. I do not tell them what I know, for they do not believe me; they just make fun of me. Well, this epidemic was terrible. We would have three funerals a day. The church bells seemed never to stop tolling. One thing made me especially sad. We buried a woman and her child together. I, too, contracted the disease, but was given some medicine to drink, which cured me. But the year after I had a relapse, and was close to death that time.

Ever anxious to get on with the business of schooling, Salpointe made arrangements with the Sisters of St. Joseph of Carondelet to send seven volunteers from St. Louis to Tucson to begin instruction at the Convent school next to San Agustín. Construction of the school had begun in 1867 and was finished, along with a house for the nuns, before 1870. The five French, one Irish, and one American sisters arrived in Tucson on Ascension Day, May 25, 1870, after a courageous journey that, in 1963, became the inspiration for a popular Hollywood movie: *Lilies of the Field*.

Apparently in anticipation of re-opening the school at San Xavier, Sister Euphrasia Suchet in 1872 prepared 28 exercises consisting of Papago-English common phrases, clauses, sentences, etc., writing them neatly on ten pages. The French teacher was clearly something of a linguist. In September 1873, she and Sister Maxime Croisat re-opened the school and were joined a month later by another Carondelet nun, the newly arrived Francesca Kelly (Cammack 1990: 2; McMahon 1952: 91, 96-97, 104-05, 112, 139-40; Salpointe 1880: 15; Suchet 1872).

At San Xavier the sisters worked initially for the U.S. Dept. of Indian Affairs under Tucson-based Dr. Reuben A. Wilbur, its agent since 1871. Their schoolhouse was the old mud adobe wing east of the church. The reconstruction of Fr. Espinosa's first church dating to 1756 was near collapse. The east wing was repaired at federal expense for use as a school, although Agent Wilbur wrote in 1873 that he had erected a "large building" for educational purposes. What seems to have happened is that Salpointe agreed to repair the building and Wilbur agreed to pay the bills from $5,000 appropriated for that purpose. Salpointe arranged for a new roof and other repairs, keeping an account of expenses in a small blank book. Wilbur supplied new doors, windows, and some furnishings (Salpointe 1875).

Knowing that he had spent only about $1,900 and that Wilbur could have spent no more than $1,500, Salpointe approached Wilbur about getting more school supplies. Wilbur, however, told him the entire $5,000 had been spent. During one of the Vicar Apostolic's absences, Wilbur "borrowed" the bishop's little expense book from one of the other priests, and later said he had lost it. Salpointe accused Wilbur of embezzlement, and their cooperation in supporting a mission school abruptly ended (Ludlam 1880; Salpointe 1875).

A series of accusations and counter-accusations between the Indian agent and the bishop culminated in Wilbur's dismissal by the government on July 2, 1874. There was no agent for the Papagos until April, when John W. Cornyn, who got along well with Salpointe, took charge. However, the Commissioner of Indian Affairs, Edward P. Smith, was a Congregationalist who didn't favor paying the Catholic Church to instruct Papagos. He was also apparently concerned with expenses, so Smith closed the San Xavier Agency on April 1, 1876, and consolidated its affairs with those of the Pimas and Maricopas on the Gila River Indian Reservation where the agents were nominated by the Dutch Reformed Church. San Xavier's school closed the same day, and its potential scholars were off on another holiday, one that would last until 1884 (Fontana 1976: 127-28, 130; Salpointe 1880: 15).

Whether Wilbur had been honest or not, he gets credit for preserving lands for the Papagos of Bac. Almost as soon as he had become their agent, he began to press hard for a reservation for the community in part because 1871 and 1872 were years of drought. In some areas the Papagos ate their livestock to the last animal as well as their seed grain (Fontana 1976: 126). But Bac was still a reliable source of water. Of the desert Papagos to the west, Wilbur reported:

As has long been their custom in the harvest season, they .... [come] from the various villages to engage as laborers in the grain fields ... It is their preference if possible to live at or near San Xavier, where they have for a long time resided and worshipped (Wilbur 1872: 321).

As Arizona Supt. of Indian Affairs, Charles Poston in 1863 had urged that a reservation be set aside, and in 1864 "made" a reservation of two square leagues (nearly 24 square miles) with San Xavier in the center. Neither Congress nor President Lincoln ever sanctioned the Poston reservation, so it lacked any legal status. Poston asked the U.S. Surveyor General for Arizona to survey the reservation and mark its boundaries, but was told that so long as Apaches were a serious threat to life and limb, the Surveyor General wasn't going to survey anything south of the Gila River (Fontana 1976: 122).

By 1874, more and more O'odham had been coming to San Xavier to take advantage of the government's issuance of farm tools and other supplies. A group of Kohatk O'odham who had been living on the Gila River with the Pimas had even asked for permission to re-settle at Bac. Thus growing numbers of people and Wilbur's persistent agitation finally had results. On July 1, 1874, President Ulysses S. Grant used his power of Executive Order to withdraw from the public

1871: San Xavier atop the facade (Timothy O'Sullivan, National Archives).

domain over 111 square miles at San Xavier for the exclusive use and occupancy of the Papagos. Wilbur had successfully argued that it would be

almost sacrilege to take them away from the church which their ancestors built ... and which owes its present state of remarkable preservation to their care and interest alone.... They built, and have protected the old mission church, which is now one of the wonders of past ages, and in every way seem peculiarly entitled to that part of the country (Fontana 1976: 128-29; 1993b: 2; 1995: 33).

Priests who signed the surviving church registers as having served at San Xavier during the first years under Salpointe of what might be called Bac's Tucson period included, by date of first entry:

J.B. Salpointe, February 1866
Francis M. M. Lestra, April 19, 1869 (burial)
Francis X. Jouvenceau, August 1869
Andrew Escallier, June 9, 1870
Antoine Jouvenceau, Sept. 22, 1872
J. M. LeClerc, April 2, 1876
Edward Gerard, April 22, 1877

May 1880: both columns are gone to the right of the balcony while to the left of the entry, the front half of that column is gone too, exposing its cottonwood core and sculpted brick (Carleton Watkins).

Minus the Santo and his coffin: the west transept with a richly garbed San Francisco de Asís above Jesús Nazareno (Edward McCain).

*The east transept with **La Dolorosa** from the 1750s first church (Edward McCain).*

Bishop Salpointe
(William A. Duffin from the book "John Baptist Salpointe – Soldier of the Cross").

With the teachers gone and no clerics in residence, some of San Xavier's treasures became the target of thieves. Early in 1880, "night robbers broke into San Xavier mission church and took the silver plate, tin and gold cruets [wine vessels], and a silver chalice, the inside of which is overlaid with gold. The intrinsic value of all the articles is not less than $500, but as relics of the old mission they are worth a much greater sum, for they are as old as the building, which must, for many years to come, be a matter of much interest to the traveler and to those who wish to study the early history of Arizona" (Miller 1962: 16).

In reaction to the theft, and because he needed money for repairs at the mission, Salpointe published a notice in the *Arizona Daily Citizen* on March 3, 1880. Henceforth, it stated, anyone wanting entry to the church would have to buy a ticket for 50 cents at the priest's residence in Tucson and present it to the sexton – probably a villager – to be admitted. The theft may also explain Salpointe's willingness to allow a licensed Indian trader employed by Tucson merchant William Zeckendorf to "occupy the building" in 1880 (Ludlam 1880; Miller 1962: 17-18).

In 1884, the Presbyterian Board of Home Missions sent a 24-year-old physician and teacher to open a school at San Xavier. Dr. F. J. Hart arrived in Tucson in August and promptly began work in a rented house near the mission. By October the Presbyterians had an agreement with the federal government that it would pay the cost of the operation, including Hart's $900 annual salary. The first term for the new day school went fairly well, and Hart reported an average daily attendance of about 15 students. He remained until October 1887, leaving his job a discouraged young man. He discovered that interesting Papagos in learning about things that have meaning only in the white man's world is not easy.

Two weeks after Hart's resignation he was replaced by another Presbyterian-appointee, J. B. Douglas. Almost at once ugly rumors circulated about Douglas, and in January 1888 he was relieved of his duties for "drunkenness and giving whiskey to the Indians." His successor, J. N. Wilson, came to San Xavier nearly a year later, in December 1888, and resigned the following August (Fontana 1976: 131).

Bishop Peter Bourgade: 1885-1899

It is unlikely that these abortive Presbyterian efforts at schooling took place in the east wing. If they did, it must have been at the displeasure of Vicar Apostolic Peter Bourgade, who succeeded Salpointe on May 5, 1885 (Nordmeyer 1978b: 41). Salpointe had left for Santa Fe on Feb. 19 to become co-adjutor to Archbishop Lamy, and on July 18 succeeded Lamy as archbishop (Faulk 1966: xiii).

Bourgade's custody of the old mission became severely strained on May 3, 1887, when an earthquake later estimated at 7.2 on the Richter scale struck at Batepito in the San Bernardino Valley in northeastern Sonora. Fifty-one Sonorans died as a result of the quake and the great adobe mission church at Bavispe was almost destroyed. Tremors were felt as far north as Prescott (DuBois and Smith 1980: 7, 28, 78).

Tucson and Bac were 140 miles northwest of the epicenter: far enough away that they were hit with only about 70 percent of the quake's maximum intensity. Before and after photographs of San Xavier indicate that the shock knocked down the atrium wall and gateway in front of the church, flattened nearly all but the eastern portions of the cemetery wall, felled the far east lower column of the façade as well as the finial atop the upper west column, and opened a floor-to-ceiling crack in the west wall of the west transept. It doubtless exacerbated already-existing cracks in the main dome and elsewhere in the building (DuBois and Smith 1980: 66-67). That the structure continued to stand at all is a tremendous tribute to the skill of its builders.

May 1880: adobe & wattle of the plaza almost all cleared away, and rebuilt adobes in front of the east tower. Scattered houses of Bac to the west (Carleton Watkins).

As shown in photos from as early as May 1887 till at least 1940, a notice the size of a business envelope above the left wicket or smaller door at San Xavier's entry warned that:

> This church is still used as a house of worship. Visitors are requested to refrain from loud talking. Gentlemen will remove their hats.

In late 1888 with the Protestants all but gone from San Xavier – much to the satisfaction of Bourgade – the Carondelet Sisters re-opened their school, this time without government support. Mother Florence Benigna O'Reilly, Sister Agnes Orosco, and Sister Mary Bernadette Smith took charge. Sister Bernadette left a record of those early days:

> When we arrived at the mission the carpenters were building a little dormitory and community room for us. Since they were not finished, we

After the May 3, 1887 earthquake (Albert S. Reynolds).

were obliged to fix up an old room in the monastery which had not been used for a hundred years or more [sic]. The first thing Mother did was get several pans of sulphur, and kept it burning in this room for several days and nights to oust the centipedes, scorpions, matavenados, tarantulas, etc., which had nested for years and years. The result was that they began to fall half-dead upon the floor, from the dried mud which formed the ceiling (McMahon 1952: 141).

The schoolrooms were ready by January 1889. Sister Bernadette was placed in charge while Mother and Sister Agnes rounded up would-be students in the village. Before long, the pupils came to enjoy their instruction (McMahon 1952: 143).

One of the teachers who soon arrived was Sister Mary Aquinas Duffy, who served at Bac for more than 40 years. The nuns wanted a chapel for their private devotions, so they cleaned up the second floor of the east bell tower, "shoveling out the dirt, dusting the walls, etc." For privacy, the sisters arranged for the second step on the stairwell up to the roof and the west end of the half-dome doorway to the choir loft to be filled in with mud adobe. That left a niche for an altar nearly five feet deep. (McMahon 1952: 142, 144). The wood base of the railing in front of the altar is still in place, but the infill adobe was removed at some point after the Historic American Buildings Survey (Sheet 6) completed in late 1940.

The bishop was short of priests to serve the growing population. Bourgade had offered to return San Xavier to the Franciscans in 1886, but they had to decline. In late 1895 the Very Rev. Michael Richardt, O.F.M., father provincial of the Franciscan Province of

1894: Sisters and pupils at the south arcade (William Dinwidie).

the Sacred Heart based in St. Louis, accepted the St. Mary's congregation in Phoenix, and, with it, care of most of the Indian tribes of Southern Arizona, including Pimas and Papagos (Engelhardt 1899: 200). But Bac still wasn't included.

In 1890, J. M. Berger had been appointed the government farmer for the San Xavier Reservation and became, in effect, the local Indian agent. Although the Papago school was privately operated, it was the only school on the reservation, so Berger clearly felt some responsibility for its maintenance. In the 1890s he and Bishop Bourgade apparently cooperated in repairing the church's

*Chief José Juan Cristóbal at
San Xavier, 1894 (William Dinwidie).*

main dome and the foundations on its south side. In 1895 the United States appropriated $1,000 for the Indian Office for repairs of mission buildings. New school rooms, largely comprising the first north-south addition to the east end of the east wing, were added in 1899 (Berger 1895, 1897, 1899, 1900, 1902, 1903, 1905; Duffy n.d.; Moore 1980; Young 1896).

Under Bourgade's tenure the only visiting priest who signed the San Xavier registers was Joseph Carnet on July 14, 1894. On Jan. 7, 1899, Bourgade became Archbishop of Santa Fe.

Putnam 1899: The crossing with benches, pews, and Victorian-framed paintings of the Stations of the Cross above the niches (Arizona State Archives).

A Saint at San Xavier

Early on the morning of Aug. 18, 1894, Bishop Peter Bourgade arrived at San Xavier with two Sisters of the Blessed Sacrament, a new order dedicated to helping Indians and blacks. One of the sisters was the 35-year-old founder and mother superior of the order. She was the heiress for life of the interest from $14 million from the then largest estate in American history, and on Oct. 1, 2000 was canonized by Pope John Paul II as St. Katharine Drexel. This is her final profession portrait taken five months after the San Xavier visit:

January 1895: The future Saint Katharine Drexel, age 36
(Archives of the Sisters of the Blessed Sacrament).

Others who have become saints may have visited San Xavier, including St. Frances Xavier Cabrini, but St. Katharine returned many times over the next 35 some years, usually stayed with the sisters at the mission school, donated considerable sums for the school as well as for renovation, and wrote requests for Mass intentions to the priests here (Morris 2014).

Bishop Bourgade had called on Mother Katharine when she was briefly in Santa Fe in April. He asked that she come to Tucson to visit the Papagos. He likely knew that in 1886, some two years before taking her initial vows, she had donated the then huge sum of $14,000 to build and furnish a Catholic boarding school in Santa Fe for Indian girls (Salpointe 1898: 273). And as the bishop was well aware, the former debutante had already contributed to San Xavier even before founding her order on Feb. 12, 1891 (Duffy 1966: 187; 269).

Mother Katharine agreed to come to Tucson, and arrived here with her companion, Sister Evangelist. While at San Xavier, she called on a friend from 1886 – J. B. Salpointe (Drexel 1894: 8, 14). Writes one of her biographers:

…. a great lover of poverty herself, (she) was keenly edified to find the retired Bishop Salpointe living in a small adobe house. The archbishop's room had a little iron bed, three yellow chairs, a crucifix on the wall, and that was all. There was no carpet, not even a small rug (Duffy 1966:187).

How much St. Katharine contributed to San Xavier is uncertain, but totals at least $5,100 – the equivalent of about $160,000 today.

In 1890, Bourgade sent Msgr. Stephan of the Bureau of Catholic Indian Missions a receipt for $1,000 for a check from Drexel & Co. for San Xavier, and a receipt for $500 in 1891.

During the 1896-97 school year she paid $300 as the salary for two sisters at San Xavier, and apparently donated another $300 in 1899.

In September 1901 she paid $1,000 to Bishop Henry Granjon for repairs, and another $1,800 in 1907 for "repairing San Xavia [sic] del Bac school for Indians near Tucson."

In 1910, she recorded having sent Sister M. Aquinas of San Xavier $25 for Christmas gifts for the children the previous year.

In 1916, she sent $200 for San Xavier to the superior, Fr. Nicholas Perschl (Morris 2014; Drexel 1902: 103, 131, & 149; Leighton 2014).

On Oct. 2 that year while staying at the mission, she wrote her sister, Louise Drexel Morrell, that San Xavier:

…. is an ideal spot. We are staying with the nuns here, in the atmosphere of the old Franciscan Mission. Their houses are wonderfully built, with walls at least two feet thick. They knew how to build for this climate. The bright sun is baking hot at 2 p.m., the time I am writing, but inside it is comfortable. One does not think of the weather at all, as one is neither too hot or too cold. There are real Franciscan Fathers in charge of the grand old Church of St. Xavier del Bac, which has been repaired by the Bishop, as in the times of the Friars of three centuries ago (Regan 2000).

Other donations by St. Katharine included $2,500 in 1912 to build Holy Family Church in Tucson, and unknown sums to help build day schools for the Papagos at Little Tucson, Comobabi, Topawa, Fresnal, Komelik and Cababi (Leighton 2014; Morris 2014).

– David Carter

Bishop Henry Granjon: 1900-1912

On April 19, 1900, Henry Granjon was appointed Bishop of Tucson. He was another French-born priest, one who served in Tombstone in 1890-92 and Prescott in 1896-97. Granjon was consecrated bishop on June 17, and in a short time threw himself vigorously into his work in Arizona Territory (Nordmeyer 1978a: 64, 66, 68; 1978b: 54).

In 1906, a committee of the Tucson Chamber of Commerce was sufficiently worried about the condition of the main dome that they commissioned an architectural study. D. H. and J. H.

Henry Granjon, Bishop of Tucson (McClintock: 1916).

Holmes reported that repairs could be made for about $150 but recommended that the "surest way to make a lasting repair, would be to put on a copper roof over the whole building and cover the dome with sheet copper. This would not mar the appearance [!!] and would last for a great many years" (Whedon 1906).

In June Bishop Granjon wrote to his friend William H. Brophy about San Xavier, noting that its Indian agent was proposing that the government open its own school on the reservation because of the deteriorating condition of the classrooms at the mission. Granjon feared that a government school would lead to the demise of the parochial school, so he set out on an ambitious project to repair not only the classrooms, but to do whatever was needed to restore

1901: The exposed east tower and circa 1810 sacristy arcade
(Gates Museum Expedition, Smylie Archives, College of Idaho).

1906: Scaffolding on the east tower before its first plaster, and at far left a volcanic rock buttress for the west bell tower. In the foreground by the horse and buggy: the start of Granjon's wall around the atrium.

he former glory of the church. He had apparently begun work on the church as early as late 1905. "One repair made another compulsory," he told Brophy, "until, after spending to date three times as much as I expected, I now find myself in the same plight as the man in St. Luke's Gospel [14:30]. This man began to build, and was not able to finish' " (Brophy 1970: 46-47).

The bishop's right hand man in this great undertaking was a superb Tucson builder, *don* Manuel G. Flores – *El Maestro* as he was called (Herreras 1981: 4). But in the second half of 1907, Granjon was still near despair: "The work seems to grow in magnitude every day, as we have reached a point where we simply have to go ahead and keep it to a finish." In August, a tremendous windstorm – the bishop called it a cyclone – damaged the arches he had been building behind the church.

His funds temporarily depleted, Granjon had to postpone the work, but by January 1908 he was back on the job, often personally wielding a shovel or trowel or paint brush – whatever it took. By August he was shopping for paint suitable to apply to the roof over the layer of concrete added to that of the 1895 repairs by Berger or Bourgade or both (Brophy 1970: 46-47).

In December 1907 Granjon had estimated that during the two years he had worked on the mission "off and on," he had spent some $11,000 – about $360,000 in 2014 dollars. And while he didn't say so, a lot of the spending was from his own money. "But it is all for God's glory," he wrote, "and the honor of the Catholic Church in America. I think those who will come after us, and write the history of the Church in Arizona, will appreciate the effort, and the sacrifices" (Brophy 1970: 47).

He was right, but renovation and more bills continued till the end of 1908, and some even later. It is fair to say that Bishop Henry Granjon's love affair with San Xavier, and it was certainly that, was its salvation. In the 1950s author Nancy Newhall summed up his accomplishments:

In 1906 there was much bustle and stir at Bac, ... *The Right Reverend Henry Granjon began to restore the mission. He covered the church and* [mortuary] *chapel with a gleaming new white coat of lime plaster, even to the unfinished tower which had always remained burnt brick. He rebuilt the balustrades of the towers ... he rebuilt the walls of the old cemetery with an entrance to the east instead of to the north, and made the walls of the atrium decorative* [as well as completely rebuilding them]; *they were no longer needed for defense, now that the Apaches were gone. Whenever he could get away from his other duties, Bishop Granjon was to be found on the scaffolding in overalls, wielding hammer and trowel alongside his workmen. Catching his enthusiasm, the Papagos managed, even after a season of bad crops, to give their Mission a new floor* [of wood], *to replace the hard* [one] *on which they had always kneeled. Church and chapel in order, Granjon went on to repair the old cloisters and* [complete] *a new wing to the east side, with an arching colonnade He enclosed the new back court with gates, including the seven-fold arch that is so impressive an addition to San Xavier's domes and towers. Apart from the new floor, it was the Bishop's own money he was spending, and San Xavier was his love and delight. He ordered finials for roof and walls ... lions' heads of thin plaster to set along the parapet where travelers had described* [the heads of] *strange beasts. He ordered* [from J.W. Fiske, Park Place, New York City] *two more* [cast metal] *lions to guard the road* [he had built] *around the little black hill, and had a* [natural] *grotto* [further] *hollowed and cemented up there to house a statue of the Virgin of Lourdes which he imported all the way from France. He bought from Mexico the image of La Soledad* [Our Lady of Solitude] ... *who stands* [in 2014 in the mission museum] *newly gorgeous in black and silver, with a lace mantilla and a star-pointed tin halo on her head and a tin heart stuck with daggers on her breast. ... To restoring Mission San Xavier and to building two churches in Tucson, Bishop Granjon happily gave all his fortune; he died a poor man* (Newhall 1954: 31-32).

1907: postcard showing the east tower nearly complete.

Edward S. Curtis 1907: Granjon's renovated façade
(Northwestern University).

*Circa 1913: the new convent at far left west of the mortuary chapel, the 1906-1907 front walls
with ball-topped finials at lower left and center, and rooms added from 1899 on at far right east of the courtyard.*

Granjon, who must have loved lions, also added a half dozen metal lions' heads on the east face of the north-south arches he built at the rear of the church. He put new finials, decidedly French in conception, atop the parapets of the church and elsewhere. He built low stone buttresses along parts of the walls of the church where salt erosion had apparently been eating at the walls. From Cincinnati he ordered the large bell for the west tower. He brought in fill north of the church and cloister so more rooms and arches could be added in that direction. And he poured a cement floor for the atrium. The bishop added a wall on the south parallel to the old east wing and, for good measure, erected a little arched entry-way at its cast end. For comfort and privacy, he built a spacious two-hole privy north of the church with seats of mahogany. Years later this outbuilding came to be known as "Granjon's jakes." Its pit was subsequently used for burning refuse, and finally the structure was torn town and the hole covered up. Today the site is under a cactus garden.

The great arch at the rear of the mission that photographer love so dearly as a frame for their pictures of the church has com to be known as Granjon's Gate. This is despite the fact that th bishop, a modest man, left his name inscribed nowhere at San Xavier. As close as Henry Granjon ever came to leaving his nam at the mission was when he recognized his position, rather than himself personally, on three marble plaques with inscriptions i Latin. The first of these, dated 1906 on the upper north side of th south arcade, reads in translation:

**THESE BUILDINGS
WERE RESTORED BY
THE BISHOP OF TUCSON**

1871: original finials & bear-like heads on the upper walls
(Timothy O'Sullivan, National Archives).

1940: Granjon's finials & lion heads
(Donald Dickensheets, Library of Congress).

Granjon's Gate at the rear of the mission (Hazel Fontana).

The 1906 marble tablet above the door of the mortuary chapel is described on page 78.

The marble tablet that Granjon mounted on the north face of his arched gateway enclosing the north side of the mission has no date. Beginning with the initials A.M.D.G. for *Ad Majorem Dei Gloriam*, the inscription translates as:

TO THE GREATER GLORY OF GOD
IN HONOR OF
ST. FRANCIS XAVIER
APOSTLE TO THE INDIES

A fourth tablet at the replica of the Grotto of Lourdes on the hill just east of the mission is in English:

ERECTED / BY THE BISHOP / OF TVCSON
A.D. 1908 / THE FIFTIETH ANNIVERSARY
OF THE WONDROVS / APPARITIONS
OF THE BLESSED / VIRGIN MOTHER / OF GOD
AT THE GROTTO / OF LOVRDES

In a very real sense, Henry Granjon saved the mission from destruction. He did it, moreover, with a deep understanding of history and with attention to preserving the architectural style.

The expenditure of large amounts of love and money by the bishop at San Xavier was made in spite of the fact that the Roman Catholic Church had no clear legal title either to the buildings or to the grounds. When the San Xavier Reservation was created in 1874 no exception was made for the church, so it became part of federal trust lands reserved for the Papagos. Nonetheless, the weight of tradition dating to Kino stood in the Church's favor. In January 1901, the Very Rev. Edward Gerard, vicar general for the Diocese of Tucson and acting as trustee for the Church, applied to the U.S. Surveyor General for a patent to 14 acres at San Xavier. The application was submitted under terms of an Act of Congress approved March 3, 1891 and its later revisions, but was rejected (Fontana 1970: 12-13).

On March 3, 1909, Congress approved another law concerning lands that might be given to religious organizations involved in mission or school work on Indian reservations, and under its terms, on May 19, 1910, President William H. Taft granted to the Bureau of Catholic Indian Missions the 14 acres on which the church stands as well as, today, the friary and adjoining structures, the school to the west, and the convent for the teaching nuns. The

patent for this island surrounded by the reservation was filed in the Pima County Recorder's Office on Aug. 13, 1910, in Book 48, page 191 (Fontana 1970: 13-14). Many years later, when the bureau closed its doors, the deed was transferred to the Diocese of Tucson. On April 11, 2006, title was transferred to the parish.

The Sisters of Carondelet had gone on the federal payroll as civil servants on March 1, 1910. The school became "public" rather than parochial, and the sisters were forbidden to teach religion. That was because Congress in the Indian Bureau Appropriations Act of 1897 had decreed that no public money could be spent for education in any church-run school (Fontana 1976: 133-34).

Visiting priests who signed the surviving San Xavier registers after Bourgade's departure and then under Granjon were:

John M. Chaucot, May 14, 1899
J. Bezamat, May 18, 1899
W. Meuer, Oct. 8, 1899
Joseph O. Barrette, Nov. 23, 1899
J. H. Cushing, April 13, 1900
Henri Granjon, March 14, 1901
J. E. Lynch, 1902
P. L. Cambiaire, Jan. 30, 1902
Frederick Derichemont, Feb. 6, 1902
Ignatius L. Brangon, March 23, 1902
Ferdinand Peitz, April 26, 1902
J. J. Donovan, Oct. 19, 1902
Francis Haase, O.F.M. (Sacred Heart Province), Nov. 16, 1902
Cypriano Vabre, Sept. 22, 1904
Aepes Quetu, October 1904
Luis Duval, Dec. 3, 1904
Emile Barrat, Dec. 21, 1904
Ferdinand Rouselle, Feb. 2, 1905
Jean Carey, Oct. 19, 1905
C. Rampont, March 26, 1907
Peter Timmermans, Nov. 29, 1907
M. Wundelich, April 19, 1908
Virgilis Genevrier, 1909
E. S. Albouy, March 14, 1909
Joseph Coulombe, May 22, 1910, and
E. Verbruggle, 1911.

The return of the Franciscans: 1912

Having invested so much in San Xavier, Granjon was reluctant to turn its administration back to the Franciscans in spite of pressure from the new owner of record – the Bureau of Catholic Indian Missions. In May 1911 he wrote to Archbishop J. B. Pitaval in Santa Fe. He argued that neither Bac's Indians nor teaching sisters nor diocesan clergy were dissatisfied with the current arrangement. It was good for his priests, he wrote, to do some missionary work. He said the diocese was willing to bear the burden of San Xavier's cost; that San Xavier was far from the western Papagos who really needed the Franciscans; and that it would make more sense to build a house for Franciscan missionaries at a place such as Casa Grande than at San Xavier. Because the sisters occupied San Xavier's living quarters, a house would have to be built for the friars wherever they went. Finally:

... San Xavier is practically Tucson, a distance of nine miles in this part of the country being counted as naught, and San Xavier being utterly tributary to and dependent on Tucson, as a suburb would be. Tucson cannot possibly entertain at present the proposition of installing a mendicant monastic Order at its doors. The progress and welfare of this Parish cannot permit it. In duty to this young and struggling Church of Arizona, neither my clergy nor myself could conscientiously consent to it (Granjon 1911).

Whether willingly or under Church orders, the bishop in 1912, the year Arizona gained statehood, put the religious supervision of San Xavier's Papagos under the Franciscans. Historian Maynard Geiger, O.F.M., notes that:

"Fr. Bonaventure Oblasser, who was already working among the desert Papagos, was appointed as their missionary. In January 1913, Fr. Tiburtius Wand, who had been laboring among the Pimas, joined Fr. Bonaventure. On Aug. 8, 1913, Fr. Ferdinand Ortiz, a native of Tucson, arrived as the first superior of the Franciscan residence. The other two fathers were thus free to labor untrammeled among the Indians of the Papaguería. In 1915, the Papaguería was removed from the jurisdiction of San Xavier, with the founding of headquarters at San Solano near Cababi" (Geiger 1939: 36).

It had been 76 years earlier, in 1837, that the last Franciscan was in permanent residence at Bac. Now the Order of Friars Minor was back.

The Franciscans who took up their duties at Bac in 1913 belonged to the Sacred Heart Province based in St. Louis. In 1915

the Saint Barbara Province was created with its headquarters in Oakland, Calif., and with Southern Arizona as part of its jurisdiction. These are the Franciscans who continue to administer the mission's affairs today (Fontana 1970: 14).

Before Fr. Ortiz arrived at Bac in 1913, friars Bonaventure Oblasser, Mathias Rechsteiner, Tiburtius Wand, and Francis Redman had already signed the registers. Soon after his arrival, Ortiz was transferred to the Apache missions and replaced by Wand whom the Papagos called "Fr. Juan," misinterpreting the pronunciation of his last name. Wand spent nearly all his time among Papagos living in the desert far to the west, so in 1916 the priest actually in residence, Fr. Nicholas Perschl, became the superior. He served till 1923, again from 1931 to 1933, and from 1939 to 1940 – 13 years in all. Other superiors and their first year in charge have been:

Francis Redman, 1923
Stephen Remer or Renier, 1925
Tiburtius Wand, 2nd term, 1927
Arnold Oscar, 1933
Marian Bucher, 1937
Ferdinand Ortiz, 2nd term, 1938
Julian Giradot, 1940
Edmund Austin, 1941
Walter Tracy, 1943
Rupert Hanner, 1944
Hermann Schneider, 1947
Celestine Chinn, 1949
Luis Baldonado, 1958
Theodore Williges, 1961
Linus Hohendorf, 1964
Kieran McCarty, 1966
Clarence Mann, 1971
Walter Holly, 1979
Michael Dallmeier, 1988
Alberic Smith, 1997
David Gaa, 2000
Stephen Barnufsky, 2003
William Minkel, 2019

Fr. Nicholas Perschl (1887-1969) in retirement at San Xavier after his three terms as superior over 13 years between 1916 and 1940 (Harry Lewis, Jack Sheaffer Photography, Arizona Daily Star).

Other priests either stationed at San Xavier or who spent considerable time here in the modern Franciscan era include, by date of first entry in the San Xavier baptismal registers:

Boniface Bartholme, 1918
Boniface Mandelartz, O.S.B., 1919
Desiderius von Trenz, 1919 [Sacred Heart Province]
Emery Kocsis, 1920 [Sacred Heart Province]
Jerome Lutenegger, 1926
Anthony Linneweber, 1928
Paul Neutkins, 1929
Andrew Bucher, 1930
Felix Pudlowski, 1932
Marcus Bucher, 1933
Robert Schmidt, 1933
Vincent Arbeiter, 1934
John Regis Rohder, 1935
Frederick Bromham, 1943

1928: In his second term as superior, Fr. Tiburtius Wand ("Fr. Juan") with, from left, a stone mason, photographer Charl Egginton, writer-researcher Prentice Duell, and a carpenter.

1928: The last ultra-baroque upper estípite column three years before its collapse (Charl Egginton).

Dennis Mahoney, 1943
John Joseph Tariel, 1944
Sebastian Dzielski, 1950
Pius Petrie, 1951
Fidelis Kuban, 1967
Capistran Hanlon, 1968
Marian Bucher, 1970
William Sisk, 1970
Lucien Pargett, 1973
Peter Krieg, 1984
Justin Moncrief, 1984
John Gini, 1995
John Gibbons, 2001
Edgar Magaña, 2002
Edward Sarrazin, 2007
Paul Wilken, 2019

In addition to the priests, there is also a long list of unsung Franciscan brothers who have served San Xavier since 1913 with great love and devotion. Bonaventure Nite, Lawrence Hogan, Berard Connolly, Christian Rogan, and Michael Bearce have been among them.

Two priests now memorialized in the mortuary chapel as the supposed followers of Garcés in the late 1770s had no connection to Bac before their reburial here on Feb. 21, 1935. It was Juan Bautista Velderrain who followed Garcés, not Baltasar Carrillo, Narciso Gutiérrez, Mariano Bordoy, and other Tumacácori priests as mistakenly cited by Salpointe (1880: 7-8). His error, one perpetuated by countless writers, resulted from the mistaken belief that some fragments of church registers were those for San Xavier rather than Tumacácori (varia). The misunderstanding led to the 1935 reburial here of the bones of Carrillo and Gutiérrez amidst much publicity. The bishop of Tucson, the bishop of Albany, N.Y., the mayor of Tucson, National Park Service officials, and many reporters were among the large crowd (Caywood 1935).

San Xavier has thrived under the Santa Barbara Franciscans. Bishop Granjon turned over to them a restored and improved mission complex. Fr. Perschl built a community hall for the Papagos (Persch 1959: 7), and in 1947 a new school was completed between the church and the convent to the west. Classrooms and shower stalls to the rear and east of the church were reused for garages, storage, and workrooms.

In March 1930, the Tucson newspapers reported the death at San Xavier of Toribio Aragon, 85, "believed to have been" the last male Sobaipuri. In December 1931, they reported the death of his widow – Encarnacion [Anton Mamake] Aragon at age 106. None of the stories define "Sobaipuri," so it's unclear whether that meant someone who spoke a dialect or accent distinct from the Tohono O'odham or whether there was some other difference or differences (*The Arizona Daily Star* 1930, 1931; *The Tucson Daily Citizen* 1930, 1931).

In 1932 to 1938 the Immaculate Heart Sisters took over the school, then the Sisters of St. Joseph of Orange. Finally, in 1940, the school was turned over to the Franciscan Sisters of Christian Charity from Manitowoc, WI. In 2014, the Franciscans continue to teach at the much-enlarged school with other religious and lay teachers. The home of the Road Runners has about 85 students in kindergarten through 8th grade (Cammack 1990: 3; San Xavier 2021).

Early in 1938, one George Marshall Crone, a supposed judge from California, took brush in hand at San Xavier with nearly disastrous results. Fr. Victor R. Stoner, an historian, wrote to Fr. Perschl on March 13 with this account:

> Somebody … bought a new can of gold paint and has done all but gild the mission itself. The cross of the Grotto Hill gleams in the setting sun. The lions of the hill have been transmuted from bronze to gold … the little cross and orb on the wall between the mission and mortuary yard is gold. And … the little tower-like ornaments atop the mortuary itself glitter and scintillate in the sun! …. Dr. Byrne (a Catholic), professor of medieval history in Columbia University … came and wept on my shoulder … He says somebody … is RETOUCHING THE PAINTINGS in the mission and spraying them with varnish. He says that the great crucifixion fresco in the sacristy is ruined.

Unhappily, not only did most of Crone's varnish blacken over time and thus obscure the original bright pigments, but in many cases it shrank and pulled off the underlying color. Outside at least, the gilding soon withered under sun and rain. In the early 1990s conservators were able to undo most of the interior damage, but not all (Patronato San Xavier 2005).

The forces of rain, wind, freezing, drying, and gravity are always at work on buildings, and San Xavier is no exception. The *Tucson Daily Citizen* reported on Aug. 28, 1931 that heavy rains from the south felled the highest and most ultra-baroque of the three remaining *estípite* columns.

On Nov. 19, 1937, the *Citizen* reported that cold had caused a large chunk of the facade, including part of the cornice, to come crashing down. Then in July 1939, lightning hit the top of the west bell tower, knocking down more than half the lantern over its dome and opening a large crack on the east face of the upper tower (*Tucson Daily Citizen*, July 24, 1939).

July 1939: west tower after lightning strike.

The lightning strike turned out to be a blessing in disguise. In February 1940, Fr. Julian Giradot invited architect and engineer Eleazar Días Herreras to the mission to see what might be done about repairing the west bell tower. With Herreras supervising and Ramón Romero doing most of the work, the lantern and tower were fully restored by the end of April. A cable attached to the lantern's iron cross was anchored into the ground as protection against future strikes (Herreras 1981: 8-10).

The entry to the baptistery with framed vestments and, in the foreground, the font from the 1750s Jesuit church.

One of the never-plastered upper stairways to the towers with fired brick as used for all the walls in the Franciscan church of the late 1700s.

April 1940: The last estípite column on the lower facade looking north. Baling wire helps hold the column in place. The second, third, and upper segments show the sculpted fired adobe behind the original lime plaster.

Baling wire to help hold up one of the last columns on the facade

June 1942: The last lower column looking east. In its center: the cottonwood core flanked by quadrants of sculpted burnt adobe laid up with fat joints of lime mortar. The northwest quadrant at left is gone – never tied into the northeast or southwest quadrants. The circa ¾-inch joints appear to be crude finish-the-work construction markedly different from the tight joints of ⅛-inch or so for the similar estípite columns in the east and west transepts. (George W. Chambers Collection, Arizona Historical Museum).

Fr. Celestine Chinn: 1949-1958

Barely five feet tall, Fr. Celestine Chinn over nine years as the superior of San Xavier, would tirelessly oversee repairs already much needed since the era of Granjon and create much of the mission as seen today. He was a successor to friars Velderrain and Llorens of the late 1700s and early 1800s in adding features to glorify God and as fast as donations could be secured. He wrote and published *Mission San Xavier del Bac*, a 24-page palm-sized guidebook that sold for years to raise funds for renovation. He completely enhanced the frontage of the old mud adobe wing east of the church. He returned ten columns to the façade. And he reconfigured the parapets. Inside the church, he arranged for the vivid over-painting of faded lower walls as well as many of the frescos, and in 1952 trimmed 10 inches off the original altar table so as "to reach into the tabernacle without train." He was attentive to detail – including a new head for the legendary plaster mouse on the façade atop the upper west scroll still across from the cat (San Xavier 1990: 69-76, 81-128).

Most of the renovation during the Chinn era was completed by outside contractors, but not all. In 1950 in an entry in the house *Chronicles* in the friar's handwriting, he reports that:

> *For the past few weeks Frs. Sebastian, Pius, and John Joseph have been engaged on various important repair jobs. By dint of hard labor and long hours, they have removed the drain pipes and repaired the cesspool at the Sisters' house; through their efforts the grease trap of the Sisters' kitchen is also in good working condition. Too much cannot be said about the interest and efforts of the said friars in putting the compound in decent shape* (San Xavier 1990: 76).

This was perhaps understatement. Barely three weeks earlier, on Oct. 3, Fr. Chinn had recorded that "Fr. Pius Petric O.F.M. arrived from Lemont, Ill. He will remain here for some time for reasons of health." On March 29, 1952, "Fr. Cletus Tripper arrived from St. Joseph's … [in Los Angeles] … Presumably for his health." But in April after the repair of a large crack in facade "running from the top to the window of the choir loft," Tripper helped Chinn repaint the façade with cement color mixed with prickly pear juice (San Xavier 1990: 75-76, 86-87).

In 1950, the piers supporting arches in the patio got a new coat of stucco and floor tiles were laid in some of the east wing rooms. In 1951, replacement balustrades were installed in the towers, and a new north patio wall was built with a new gate. Early in 1952 the façade's two surviving *estípite* columns in storage, encased in archaeological plaster since mid-1942, were at last shipped gratis

"The Bell Tower, Lion Heads and Finials"
Photograph by Ansel Adams, mid-1953
© 2014 The Ansel Adams Publishing Rights Trust.

Volute parapets similar to those at Caborca, Sonora, were added in 1954 along with finials in the original style replaced by Bishop Granjon circa 1906. (David Carter: 2013).

1902: the 1873-1958 facade east of the church
(Detroit Publishing Co., Library of Congress).

The 1958 facade with neo-baroque portada and cornice (David Carter).

to Los Angeles by Tucson Warehouse & Transfer. Sculptor J. S. Watkins made molds to cast concrete replicas for all ten columns on the façade similar to the cast stone he installed in the late 1920s on the Pima County Courthouse. Also in 1952, the corner volute buttresses on the bell towers were repaired and John Berger's weather-eroded balconies of 1895 were replaced.

The newly cast replicas for the façade's *estípite* columns were installed in February 1953. Late that same year Tucson artist Henry Milan began to "restore," actually to overpaint in oil, a half dozen large murals on the lower level of the church's interior as well as the pastel geometric dado or wainscot at the base of the walls and the *trompe l'oeil* "wood" doors.

For a month beginning on March 29, 1954, the crumbling plaster lion heads at the top of the church parapets flanking the piers supporting the finials were replaced with volute scrolls of hard brick covered with new plaster. Architect E. D. Herreras designed the volutes to resemble those at Caborca, San Xavier's sister mission. The house *Chronicles* attribute the lion heads as well as the

Sculptor J. S. Watkins in his El Presidio studio with castings for the existing columns on the facade. (George W. Chambers Collection, Arizona Historical Museum).

octagonal finials to Bishop Granjon circa 1900-1906 (San Xavier 1990: 100-101). The 1940 HABS drawings date Granjon's finials to about 1910. Herreras apparently did not have access to high-resolution enlargements of the 1871 Timothy O'Sullivan photo showing what appear to be the heads of bears on the parapets.

Later in 1954 the church roof was re-plastered and white-washed, the mortuary chapel repaired and white-washed, and Granjon's wooden flooring in the church replaced with terra cotta tiles set on a cement slab. In 1955, a similar tile floor was laid in the sacristy.

There was a lull in the activity until early 1958 when the entire east-west wing south of the patio – Fr. Espinosa's simple 1750s church in its post-1797 location – was renovated as faux Baroque. The basic territorial style with wood-cased doors and windows and a sloping tin roof were replaced with an ornate entry, wall drains as on the church, and parapets with a major cornice and sub-cornice to conceal the roof. Architect William Y. Peters had designed the new façade two years earlier. The *Chronicles* describe the doorway and the framing around the windows as intended to be decorative, but in the end a structural help in supporting the "truly wretched" walls of river-silt adobes and similar mortar (San Xavier 1990: 114-115, 124-125).

The skilled craftsmen who worked on these projects included Apolino Morales, Gilberto Sánchez, Porfirio Duarte, Fernando Pacheco, Pilar Caceres, Sid Hillings, and Ray Siquieros. Blacksmith J. W. Barlow made seven iron window grilles, and blacksmith extraordinaire Raúl Vásquez contributed decorative iron handle

Circa 1956: sacristy towel hanger by Raúl Vásquez (Edward McCain).

for the front doors of the church in the shape of a rattlesnake and a mouse (Soto 1964). About the same time, Vásquez also designed and crafted a horse-head figure with fangs holding a ring for towels next to the wash basin built into the south wall of the sacristy (Fontana 2010).

Fr. Luis Baldonado, who succeeded Chinn as superior, discovered in 1959 that Granjon's arched gateway at the rear of the mission was tilting precariously. Apolino Morales's crew tore down most of the mud adobe arch and replaced it with brick. Before the mortar could set, a big windstorm caused serious damage, and it was mid-August before final repairs were complete (Foster 1969: 17-18).

The importance of Mission San Xavier to America's heritage was officially recognized on Oct. 9, 1960 when the U.S. Dept. of the Interior through the National Park Service declared it a Registered National Historic Landmark.

One of the most celebrated of countless paintings of the mission: Ted DeGrazia's 1960 oil, "Fiesta at San Xavier." (DeGrazia Foundation).

An afternoon tornado on Aug. 27, 1964 killed a mother and infant, injured eight others, destroyed six houses as well as the convent, and damaged the school (*Tucson Daily Citizen*, Aug. 28, 1964, pages 1 & 2). Most of the upper walls and roof of the 1913 convent were torn off. The remaining structure had to be demolished. A new convent was built in late 1965.

For just over 275 years since Kino's founding of San Xavier, every Mass at Bac was celebrated in Latin. On Oct. 22, 1967, Mass for the first time was celebrated in English. Over the next few weeks, Fr. Kieran McCarty experimented with a new altar: not at the *reta-lo mayor* in the recess of the sanctuary, but under the great dome

in the midst of the congregation. In May, the provisional altar was replaced by a concrete altar designed and built by contractor James Metz.

Since fall, Metz, under McCarty's supervision, had installed new wiring in many parts of the church and adjoining buildings; improved the library, recreation room, office, and gift shop; and undertaken a fairly major attempt to clean much of the church's interior. Metz patched exterior cracks in the wall, replaced plaster on the lower level of the façade, and painted the entire church exterior for the first time since 1959. In the patio he built a fountain based on a design by Hazel Fontana and drawn by landscape architect Warren Jones (Foster 1969: 18-22). Metz also made a mold from one of Granjon's French finials and in June 1970 recast a new set of them to top the parapet. These, however, were replaced in 1985 with concrete finials cast in the original 18th-century Spanish form.

On Oct. 29, 1971, the federal government again honored San Xavier, this time via the U.S. Post Office on a new stamp as part of four stamps representing historic preservation.

In late 1973, a thief or thieves stole a large statue of San Xavier believed to be probably French and dating to between 1850 and 1925. The cast-plaster figure had appeared in both transepts, in the *sotocoro*, and at least once as seen in a circa 1940s photograph in the niche above the tabernacle, which is ordinarily the home of the San Xavier ordered from Mexico City in 1759 by Fr. Espinosa (Ahlborn 1974: 110; copy of a photo in the parish office).

In February 1974, two villagers received permission from Fr. Clarence Mann to "repair" the long-headless statue of San Xavier at the top of the façade. They cemented a metal pipe in the top of the statue so that a large red and green flag with the initials SFX can fly above the façade on and around Dec. 3, the patron's feast day. But in so doing, almost all of the robed statue except for the lowest portions to the rear were covered in plaster – leaving a sort of rounded, upside-down cone of cement.

Non-original San Xavier stolen in late 1973 (Donald. W. Dickensheets, Library of Congress).

San Xavier statue as seen till 1974
(Charl Eggington)

San Xavier is remarkably little changed since the 1700s, but part of that original legacy was lost on the morning of Aug. 6, 1982. The pair of smiling wooden lions on the altar railings guarding the entry to the sanctuary had apparently been stolen. Happily, Tucson art conservator Gloria Giffords and her husband Spencer came to the rescue. They showed photographs and measured drawings of the original lions to Jorge and Héctor Ortega, third-generation carousel builders in Puebla east of Mexico City. These expert woodcarvers sculpted new lions out of ahuehuete (*Taxodium mucronatum*), and the lions were then brought to Gloria Giffords's studio to cure for two years. As the wood dried, cracks appeared, which Giffords filled with rabbit-skin glue, whiting, and strips of wood. She covered joints and seams with strong silk and more rabbit glue, then applied gesso, bole, gold leaf, diluted acrylic paint, and white shellac. In applying the gold leaf, she would wave each stamp-size piece next to her gold-flecked electrostatic bouffant hairdo nearly two feet in diameter. The resulting charge helped in burnishing the gold leaf into the new faces, manes, and tails. The replacement lions, excellent replicas and donated by the Giffords, were installed in the church on July 17, 1988, when they were publicly blessed (Giffords 1990: 19, 21, 25-29).

The mystery as to how the original lions had vanished was solved in 2000 when the friar who had been the superior in 1982 received a letter from an itinerant to whom the Franciscans had given a temporary job as a custodian. The man confessed that, suffering from paranoid schizophrenia, he removed the lions early one morning and burned them in an incinerator behind the mission, then walked away, leaving San Xavier (Fontana 2010: 160).

On Jan. 22, 1986, by a vote of 1,236 to 944, the Papago Reservation including its San Xavier District became the Tohono O'odham Nation under a new constitution (Duarte 1986: 1D). Today at Wa:k, villagers with renewed interest in their riverine heritage distinguish its Sobaipuri traditions from those of the desert Tohono

Left: old and new city seals depicting San Xavier. Right: county seal.

The new right lion installed in 1988. To create an antique appearance, conservator Gloria Giffords applied gesso and gilding, and adjusted the color and varnish (Edward McCain).

at Sells and the 10 districts to the west. Mission San Xavier is foremost, the parish church for the residents of the San Xavier District of what today is the Tohono O'odham Nation (parish boundaries and district boundaries are the same). The Mission is also the preferred place of worship for many local Hispanic and Anglos. Beyond that, San Xavier is a symbol of community identity. The church is prominent on the city and county seals. The mission with the never-finished bell tower has also become internationally renown, attracting each year thousands of tourists, photographers, and other visitors from throughout the world. In that sense, it has become a place of worship and wonderment that belongs to everyone.

The Patronato San Xavier: 1978

In June 1978, a group of Tucsonans led by attorney James M. Murphy and whose other members were Emil W. Haury, Diann Bret Harte, Jane H. Ivancovich, Watson Smith, and Bernard L. Fontana, incorporated the Patronato San Xavier. The non-profit corporation is "to be used solely and exclusively for historical, research, scientific and educational purposes concerned with the restoration, maintenance and preservation of Mission San Xavier del Bac near Tucson, Arizona ..." (Patronato San Xavier 1978).

The financial burden of the conservation and maintenance of the mission structures and artifacts had clearly become too burdensome for either the Diocese of Tucson or the Franciscans. The church and the Franciscans in particular seek to address human needs that take priority over concerns for the material integrity

1994: Conservators find that the supposed Christ as the Good Shepherd or Buen Pastor on the north wall of the drum below the main dome is actually yet another Marian image, in this case of the Divina Pastora as first envisaged in 1703 in Seville (Edward McCain).

The triangular corner pendentives, drum, and main dome rise over 50 feet above the crossing where the nave meets the transepts and continues to the sanctuary. The image at left of the Divine Shepherdess is just above the bottom arch. The bishop shown on page 63 is at the upper left (Edward McCain).

of historic buildings. Accordingly, and because San Xavier is an open, active church every day of the year and thus cannot receive taxpayer dollars, the Patronato was organized as a non-sectarian, broadly based greater Tucson organization whose members serve as volunteers (Fontana 1993a).

Since 1978 the Patronato has raised over $14 million to pay for studies of the condition of the church and its art (Giffords & Celorio 1985; Holben & Lawrence 1985); for exterior repairs and maintenance under five generations at Morales Restoration & Builders since the 1940s; and, from 1992 to 1997, for annual three-month campaigns of interior stabilization, cleaning, and presentation of the painted and sculptural art. A team of international conservators coordinated by Paul Schwartzbaum of the Guggenheim Museum included the prestigious and experienced Rome-based conservation firm headed by Carlo Giantomass and Donatella Zari. Working with them were Italians Mario Pulieri, Vincenzo Centanni, and Paola Zari in Pulieri, as well as Turkish conservator Ridvan Isler.

In 1992, these experts began training four San Xavier Tohono O'odham in conservation techniques that they might become professionally qualified

1993: Gabriel Wilson cleaning the statue of San Francisco de Asís in the west transept (Helga Teiwes).

2014: Conservators Matilde Rubio and Tim Lewis.

to become the expert caretakers of the church. The young men with the most training were Tim Lewis, Gabriel Wilson, Donald Preston, and Mark Lopez. Lewis and Wilson went on to work on other notable projects – especially Lewis. Over the last 28 years he has divided his time between conservation work in Europe and ongoing restoration and specialized maintenance conservation at San Xavier. In Salzburg he met fellow conservator Matilde Rubio. After a visit here they decided to marry, so both have been able to help here with the never-ending work of keeping pigments and plaster intact despite the ravages of underlying salts that swell and fester because of our heat and humidity. Other issues include removing the nests of mud-dauber wasps in all sorts of crevices and using a specialized vacuum to safely clear away dust swept in at the start of summer storms. Without regularly scheduled care of every inch of the interior, dust can build up into a difficult to remove crust while masking the renewal of the conservators in the 1990s. As proposed by Schwartzbaum, there has been no interior restoration – no replacement of missing plaster or over-painting, but just the cleaning, re-adhesion, and otherwise uncovering of the original pigments and textures (Fontana 1995, Patronato San Xavier 1991).

After years of discussion and sometimes contentious planning, new living quarters were erected for the friars at the rear of the church. The friary, built in two stages between September 1990 (the north wing) and October 1994 (the west wing), was designed by architect Bob Vint, who is also the Patronato's architect, and built by the Morales company. The mission, as always, continually adapts to the times and circumstances. In 1995, for example, the moisture-weakened mud adobe piers and arches probably dating from 1874 on the north side of the old wing east of the church were replaced with new piers and arches of cement block with steel reinforcing bars grouted inside by the Morales company. The result was a perfect exterior copy of the originals, but with seismic and seepage resistance that will last indefinitely.

Architect Bob Vint
(Marcellus Rusk).

In December 1995, under the choir loft – the *sotocoro* – light was added with the installation of a silver chandelier made by Tucsonan Joe Harris and suspended on three chains in the form of plants and animals as designed by Betty Harris and other local metalsmiths. The chandelier is modeled after those painted high on the east wall of the east transept (Fontana 2010: 47-49). In the same year, Pierini Jewelers of Tucson made a mold from the gold earring found in the dust below the *Inmaculada* in the sanctuary. Now both of her pierced ears wear matching earrings except the original has a Venetian glass pendant and the replica a freshwater pearl (Fontana 2010: 181).

Over 1,500 parishioners, conservators, donors, and other supporters including Bishop Manuel Moreno celebrated the renovation of the church and the 200th anniversary of its completion on April 12, 1997. Finishing touches in the interior were completed the next month, returning the art and architecture close to its late 1700s splendor. In July the Arizona Historical Society opened an exhibit on "Angels of Restoration." In October the Tucson Museum of Art invited artists to submit images or interpretations of San Xavier for a similar special exhibit. In December with the help of singer Linda Ronstadt as honorary chair and surprise guest soloist from the choir loft, a Christmas concert raised $10,000 for exterior renovation. Grayson Hirst of the Sons of Orpheus Men's Choir and Julian Ackerley of the Tucson Boys Chorus led and still lead the benefit, which has grown over 23 seasons to seven close-to-sold-out votive-lit concerts each year (Patronato San Xavier 1997, 1998).

The 1997 spoiler, as in 1939, was lightning. A bolt again blasted the west tower, this time on Aug. 24 at 1 in the morning. The grounding cable carried most of the charge to grade, but in three spots on the north side was torn from its anchors, leaving holes 6 to 8 inches in diameter. The lowest hole drilled through two feet of brick. Portions of the tower cornice under the northwest volute buttress were further loosened and needed emergency anchorage by the Morales company. The mission's phone and sound system were destroyed, and most of its electrical system (Fontana 2006: 31).

David Gaa, a Franciscan since 1990, became the first priest ordained at San Xavier on Aug. 8, 1998. In 2000 he became the pastor, serving here till March 1, 2003 when he transferred to duties in Kazakhstan and was succeeded by Fr. Stephen Barnufsky (PSX 2000, 2003).

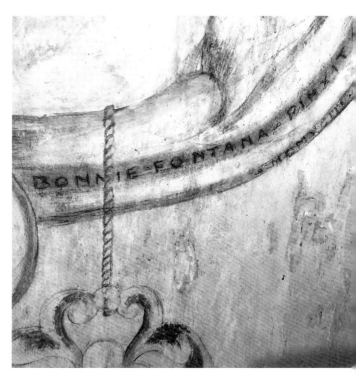

April 1993: Over 25 feet above the church floor and too small to be seen from there, Italian conservator Donatella Zari left a note to history about an inch high in watercolor and in Latin. She recorded that the secretary of the Patronato San Xavier, sponsor of the conservation, had prodded her to paint in the faint, almost missing cord figuratively holding the mural below on the upper south wall of the west transept. In English: "Bunny Fontana painted this 1993" (Fontana 2010: 265). (David Carter).

Grayson Hirst conducts the Sons of Orpheus while, seated, the Tucson Boys Chorus awaits its turn. The December concerts are a major fundraiser for renovation. "O Holy Night" caps each performance, with a slow, soft "Silent Night" as the recessional led by candle-carrying girls from Bac (James F. Palka © 2010).

The 25 cast concrete replicas of the original finials atop San Xavier's parapets weighed 293 pounds each. Patronato consultants feared that even nominal tremors might dislodge one of them, so Morales Restoration & Builders, now under Danny Morales as successor to his father Sonny and grandfather Apolino, began replacing the 1985 finials with fiberglass versions. They looked virtually identical but weighed only a few pounds apiece (PSX 2000).

October 2014: Sonny, Danny, and Vince Morales – the third, fourth, and fifth generations of their family to preserve and protect San Xavier (David Carter).

The interior of the mortuary chapel was spray painted and modern plaster statues brought by petitioners for divine help were smashed to pieces late on the night of Feb. 12, 2001 or early the next morning. The Morales company erased the graffiti under team pressure and later iron gates were installed at the entry in addition to the mahogany doors from 1954. Some called for guards around the clock, but Fr. Gaa elected to instead install surveillance cameras (Morlock 2002: 1A-2A).

The ponderous Metz altar installed in 1968 had been removed in October 2000 and replaced temporarily by a more portable wooden altar. Today's sabino wood altar and its matching candlesticks, lectern, ambo, and credence table were installed in July 2002. The furnishings were commissioned by Patronato board member Ann Fallon, designed by Rory McCarthy, and crafted by Ed Clay.

Renovation of the west tower began in late September 2002. The Patronato had a bit over $360,000 in hand to cover costs, but voted to proceed and raise funds as the work progressed over an estimated four years at a tab of circa $1.5 million. Legions of photographers were livid when scaffolding and then protective shade mesh shrouded the west tower, but renovation was the first priority.

About a year of side work on the school and elsewhere delayed completion of the west tower, but the chief obstacle to meeting deadlines as on generic construction was that the Morales crew had no way of knowing how much repair would be needed till up to a century of cement plaster could be carefully removed. Two of the three volute buttresses had to be rebuilt and so did the lantern over the dome to return it to its original orientation before the 1939 lightning strike (PSX 2005).

Cement plaster is strong but rigid. It cracks under thermal expansion and contraction, opening the underlying burnt brick and lime mortar to rain. In the winter, ice can widen the fissures.

A bishop – perhaps St. Ambrose of Milan (ca. 340-397) – in the southwest pendentive between the archways from the nave and the west transept. This transition from the large arches supports an octagonal drum with its quatrefoil windows and, above that, the main dome (Edward McCain).

The flower-filled domed ceiling of the east transept as it appeared before decades of water damage. Conservator intern Svitlana Hluwko of Ukraine devoted hours on high scaffolding in 1992 to studying the smattering of remaining pigments and charting the positions of the low-relief flowers to create this watercolor. The Patronato hopes that similar efforts someday can show us the original ceilings of the west transept and the sanctuary.

Water penetrates behind the cement overlay but can't readily evaporate away as with softer and more flexible lime plaster. The original Franciscans at Bac used lime, sand, water, and a binder extracted from the juices of the prickly pear. That's the mortar again used today for multiple thin layers of exterior plaster and to repoint underlying brick where the original lime mortar has been eroded or damaged. Technical tip: fresh, plump *nopal* or prickly pear pads are dropped into the lever-handled mop press on a basic janitor's bucket, then squeezed tight as the juice collects in the bucket.

Burnt brick is imported from Querobabi near Santa Ana, Sonora. Baluster centers were cored layer by layer and handrail undersides grooved to grout around ¾-inch fiberglass rods – reinforcing stronger than steel and with zero conductivity when lightning strikes again. The west tower and other parts of San Xavier are now structurally stronger than ever due to this hidden help within the finished renovation.

In October 2005, Lorrraine Drachman, a Patronato board member for 13 years with countless volunteer hours, retired as development director. Major donations she obtained included two $250,000 federal grants – from the Save America's Treasures program under the National Park Service, and from the Dept. of Housing & Urban Development. Drachman was succeeded by Vern Lamplot, a former television reporter with long experience at the University of Arizona. In 2007 he was named executive director (PSX 2004, 2006).

Initial studies of the last major area of exterior renovation – the ornate façade between the bell towers – began on Feb. 15, 2008. Anthony Crosby, then a Denver-based preservation architect, studied the façade top to bottom via San Xavier's small lift and then a large boom lift provided by Tucson Electric Power. Conservators Tim Lewis and Matilde Rubio began a months-long survey of the surfaces later that year from temporary scaffolding. And in February 2011, physicist and lightening consultant Leon Byerley analyzed the risks of the steel reinforcing installed in the 1950s columns and the 20 steel straps anchoring the columns to the original façade (Crosby 2008; Lewis and Rubio 2008; Vint 2011: 1-4).

Long-delayed renovation of the baptistery at the base of the west tower led to a stunning discovery on March 20, 2008. Conservators Lewis and Rubio were removing a century-old overcoat of grime and plaster residue on the north wall. Over the last three years as time allowed they had been painstakingly renovating the domed ceiling and walls. They had seen the outline of an angel, but suddenly a second angel began to appear in front of the first. Both appear to be watching over San Juan as he baptizes Christ. All of the figures appeared to be mere outlines – perhaps never-completed initial sketches from the late 1700s. But the conservators slowly and patiently uncovered skin tones, cloak colors, and cloak folds of a substantially more finished painting. The emergence of the second angel brought the total still extant at San Xavier to 183 (PSX 2008).

Renovation of the west tower was completed just before the 2008 Christmas concerts. The cost was about $2.5 million. But on Feb. 2, just a month before work was to begin on the east tower, financially strapped state officials ordered all recipients of Heritage Fund grants to cease work. The Legislature re-directed all the funds, including $150,000 awarded to the Patronato, to cover expenses in the midst of the economic downturn (PSX 2009).

Work shifted to the circa 1810 sacristy arcade east of the church. The Morales crew removed some three feet of 1950s heavy grouted parapets blocking the view of the sacristy dome. Ditto for water-eroded mesquite beams about to collapse due to long-undetected leaks at the southwest corner of the courtyard. Below grade, the east walls of the old chapter room and east transept were stabilized and repaired. Side piers 16 inches square were added inside each of the piers between the arcade arches to reduce seismic risk. They also help support a new roof with heavy joists pocketed into the original fabric but hidden above saguaro ribs reinstalled over the original mesquite ceiling beams.

2013: A late discovery

San Xavier is a gift that keeps on giving. On Dec. 12 after the 8 p.m. start of the last of the year's Christmas concerts, the night lighting projecting upward on the façade helped disclose seven figures in the folds of the scallop shell above the choir loft window. This was the view –

Figures in the façade's scallop shell, attribute of Santiago (Charles Albanese).

David Carter, the editor of this history, was chatting about plans for façade renovation with Martín DeSoto, a new colleague on the Patronato, when he noticed the figures. Carter quickly asked DeSoto and others if they too could see the images. All agreed that there appear to be similar-size standing figures. In daylight they are difficult or impossible to see because even at noon on the winter solstice, the sun is still high enough to shadow much of the shell. Years of exposure have erased much of the pigment, but the Patronato hopes that high-resolution photos and other analysis will reveal more details. The shell is the emblem of St. James the Greater – of Santiago, the patron saint of Spain. The central figure may be Christ looking to Santiago on the right.

Thanks to architectural detective work, contractor Dann Morales discovered that the south doors at the museum entry f exactly into the old askew jambs in the doorway to the chapte room. The doors have been repaired and moved back to their original site. The arcade will help protect them from rain and solar exposure. The arcade work cost more than $1 million and continued into 2014, but allowed time to raise initial funds for, finally, the east tower (PSX 2010-2014).

Until March 2020, with the start of the Covid-19 pandemic, Mass was celebrated each weekday at 6:30 a.m. in the east end of the rebuilt first church - in the small chapel created by Fr. Michael Dallmeier in 1995. He converted what by then had become its large east room into a chapel, which now is named in honor of San Juan Diego, witness in 1531 to apparitions of the patroness of Mexico – *la Virgen de Guadalupe*. The remaining three rooms in the east wing are used for a video and photographic history of renovation; a reception area in the zaguán at the entry to the museum where low-soot votive candles are on sale and visitors may obtain brochures about San Xavier; and the first rooms of the museum.

October 2014: A partial view of the newly installed pine doors opening from the old chapter room to the sacristy arcade. The doors are back in their original location for the first time since as early as 1906. From at least 1940 the doors were hung at the entry to today's museum on the south frontage east of the church (David Carter).

(left) June 2014: The southeast corner of the main cornice of the east tower before emergency stabilization by Morales Restoration & Builders (Bob Vint).

Fall 2014: Docent/parishioners Tony and Pat Doughty update Fr. Stephen Barnufsky on the latest volunteers to qualify for leading free tours of the church and museum on Mondays through Saturdays. Pastor for 16½ years from 2003 to Sept. 1, 2019, Fr. Barnufsky lauded the docents for helping introduce visitors to the parish's history, art, and architecture. There is no set script: each docent emphasizes areas of particular personal interest while still covering the major topics – and fielding questions of all sorts. The first docents met in February 2011. Under the initial direction of Vern Lamplot, executive director of the Patronato San Xavier, and Coordinator Al Lockwood, the docents till Covid organized each fall a rigorous background class for prospects, requiring that the successful candidates shadow tours by five of the current docents before leading a tour on their own (David Carter).

Emergency stabilization on the tower in June 2014 removed chunks of cornice ready to collapse on the southwest corner. In June 2013 over nine feet of the north side of the same cornice collapsed in the middle of the night, but fortunately on top of the sturdy chapter room vaults. The Morales crew initially will complete the stabilization of the lower walls (Vint 2013).

Perversely, the 2014 stabilization partially masks the previously glaring need for renovation. Potential donors have to look hard at the top of the east tower and elsewhere to see irregular, still-unrepaired cornices and other ragged details. The temporary overlays of white plaster keep bricks and mortar in place, but on first glance blend in with other areas needing no immediate attention.

The Feast Committees:
O'odham oversee church / community celebrations

The Feast of San Francisco at San Xavier was in successful operation yesterday, and the full programme was carried out, including bull fight and all. A feast day in Arizona comprehends a great deal more than a square feed.

– The Daily Arizona Citizen, Dec. 4, 1879

Fireworks beginning hours before dawn, bands, chants, bell-ringing, processions, dancing, and barbecues mix with Masses in early December to celebrate the saint's day or feast day of San Francisco Xavier. This is the culmination of joint Catholic and O'odham celebrations at Christmas, New Year's, Corpus Christi, and in early October on the feast day of the other Francisco, St. Francis of Assisi.

In 1896, Archbishop Salpointe and Bishop Bourgade celebrated a Pontifical High Mass as part of ceremonies attended by 1,200 Papagos and 600 Tucsonans (*The Arizona Daily Star* 12-5-1896: 4). But then and up to recent years, the 12 village men of the current Feast Committee plan and pay for everything else, slaughter a steer for the feasting, and at the finale turn over their duties to a new committee for the year to come. Twelve women now also directly join in leading the festivities instead of helping in the background.

The new chairman accepts the cane of office – a black wood cane about a yard long with red, white, purple, and yellow ribbons tied below a large, intricate gold top inscribed *St Xavier pray for us.* Local tradition says the cane was given to the mission by Lincoln (*The Arizona Daily Star* 12-3-1929: 3), but canes of honor and office date to Padre Kino's apostolate. At his behest, Lt. Juan Mateo Manje presented canes decorated with ribbons to chiefs and headmen in villages en route west

to Magdalena in early February 1694. Later in Caborca, Kino performed the honors, bestowing beribboned canes to local headmen (Bolton 1936: 272-273).

Behind an altar boy carrying a brass crucifix and other young villagers, the Feast Committee carries a flower-trimmed domed canopy sheltering the statue of San Xavier ordered in 1759 from Mexico City. Usually the San Xavier presides over the first niche above the tabernacle on the main altar – the *retablo mayor.* But on Dec. 2 and 3 he stands at the crossing below the main dome, then is carried outside. Priests and sisters join in the procession, as well as Yaqui dancers, local bands, parishioners, and visitors. When the saint and the procession leave the church, all the old bells begin tolling and fireworks erupt above Grotto Hill, both continuing non-stop till San Xavier again returns to the church.

For much of the 1900s, the procession slowly paraded east up Grotto Hill carrying candles, passing the Shrine of Our Lady of Lourdes, circling around the top of the hill, then returning to the plaza and the church. In recent years with a new plaza in front of the church, the processions circle counter-clockwise around the black volcanic rocks outlining dragging coyote – the center of the plaza.

– David Carter

Circa 1938: San Xavier carried in his flowered canopy as his feast-day procession rounds Grotto Hill in early December (J. Robert Burns, The Arizona Daily Star).

Marian procession in 1953 (Arizona Historical Museum #62757).

In 2015, conservators Tim Lewis and Matilde Rubio clean and stabilize the sanctuary's east murals, a year after conserving the murals on the west wall – their first full renovation since the mid-1990s. The sanctuary is more than 80 feet from the main entry where most of the dust blows into the church, but over almost 20 years and even high up, dust accumulates and hardens, making it difficult to remove. In 2016 the conservators turn to the main altar.

In the old chapter room, contractor Danny Morales and team continue stabilization begun in late 2014 at the south wall – the north wall of the east tower. The crew excavates to the andesite conglomerate bedrock below the wall. Old crumbly mortar between the foundation stones is removed, small gaps repointed with lime mortar, while below and in front of the lower stones a grid of fiberglass rebar is grouted in limecrete – a lime-sand mix that over about nine months becomes as hard as concrete but with zero cement.

Above, old plaster is removed up to the arched top of the south wall, unveiling a notable discovery. Over the doorway at far right into the east tower, the Franciscans built a flat arch of angled burnt brick abutting the outside wall of the nave. The base of the half-round recess in the center of the wall shows the basic design of the church walls – low-fired brick as a veneer, and within volcanic rock rubble dumped into a wet mix of lime and sand that turns almost as hard as rock (PSX 2014, 2015; R. Vint 2-18-2015).

New solid mesquite doors at the museum entry installed by Santiago Garcia, Vince Morales, and Danny Morales in June 2015. Master carpenter Tim Hulette built the doors and Patagonia blacksmith Richard Connolly fashioned the hinges as well as the lock (PSX 2015) (Martín DeSoto).

The flat arch at right in the north wall of the east tower functions as an arch and survived the 1887 quake, but in 2015 was again plastered to protect the bricks. The arched niche is still visible behind plate glass (David Carter).

In May 2015, Miles Green takes office as the new executive director of the Patronato. Raised and educated in New Zealand with a degree in psychology, he has lived in Tucson since 1988, working in clinical services, education, and business. Fundraising into 2015 totals $800,000 for renovation, including proceeds since 2009 from spring concerts in late afternoons (PSX 2015).

On Oct. 15, San Xavier becomes one of 50 cultural heritage sites in 36 countries named to the 2016 World Monuments Watch. The mission is praised for reversing many inappropriate repairs while continuing as a parish church. But less than three weeks later a setback: county voters reject plans for $815 million in bonds, including a 3-2 margin against $2.5 million for renovation of the east tower and the façade (Pima County 2015).

On Jan. 12, 2016, at Mission San Luis Rey, the Franciscan province of St. Barbara elects Fr. David Gaa, San Xavier's pastor from 2000 to 2003, as provincial minister of its 165 friars in Arizona, California, Oregon, and Washington. A Catholic convert at age 24, Gaa is to serve a 6- to 9-year term. His new vicar provincial or chief assistant is Fr. Martín Ibarra, O.F.M., who also served at San Xavier (St. Barbara Province). In March, Simon & Schuster brings welcome publicity with five pages on San Xavier in

La Inmaculada newly cleaned by Tim Lewis and Matilde Rubio and again in her niche in the sanctuary in May 2016. Trios of red roses on double-leaf green stems adorn the niche, but only where visible from below. See page 76 for an overall view more than 15 years earlier (Matilde Rubio).

50 Great American Places: Essential Historic Sites Across the U.S. by Brent D. Glass, former director of the Smithsonian's National Museum of American History.

By summer, lighting engineer Chris Monrad begins to restore top-quality lights to the interior. High-heat flood lamps are replaced with warm but low-profile and longer-lasting lights. In September, Susie Moreno of Wa:k begins training as an apprentice conservator. Her first assignment is cleaning and repairing the lower portions of the *retablo mayor*. On Nov. 4, the chapter room re-opens. Most of the fired brick of the south wall including the flat arch is again under lime plaster. That's so hands-on visitors won't erode the brick, but the masonry of the arched recess can still be seen behind protective plate glass (PSX 2016, Fall 2016).

Late in 2016, the Morales crew moves from the chapter room into the short passage to the first floor of the east tower, the first floor, and the first room east of the tower. Initial work again focuses on the foundations. Most of the floor is brick on sand and easy to remove. The tower's east wall needs much more removal of crumbly mortar and loose rock. In the room to the east much of the south wall mud adobe needs to be replaced (PSX Board 1-19-2017).

2017: Saving original and early wood

In June 2017, a conservation student approaches Lewis and Rubio about their work on saving the wobbly wood altar railings at the entry to the sanctuary. He volunteers to help, and the two conservators readily accept, although not yet knowing the background of Luke Addington, a French-trained specialist in antique furniture repair and collector of hundreds of ancient handmade tools. The native Tucsonan returns a few minutes later in lab coat, blue gloves, and carrying a metal briefcase neatly packed with modern tools.

Black to green and black-red to red: a cleaning test in February 2017 removes grime and overpainting on the altar handrail (Tohono Restoration).

Removal of years of accumulated dust and over-painting had revealed vivid original colors, but repair of the base was still a challenge because of termite damage. Addington is able to save some of the wood, then craft custom molds that allow for replicating the base with infill epoxies to the original contours (PSX Fall 2017).

Luke Addington repairs altar rail base (Matilde Rubio).

Under contract with the Patronato, Addington next saves five beams of ponderosa pine from the ceiling of the adobe room east of the east tower. Between September 2017 and January 2018 he analyzes each beam, finding markings in the surviving surfaces showing that they had been hewn with stone or metal adzes and hatchets. He extracts termite-damaged wood beyond repair as well as larvae and other insects while retaining every possible portion of each beam. After treating the pine with borates to protect against insects in years to come, Addington injects penetrating epoxies into the crevices and voids, adds layers of more epoxy, and finally shapes the tinted structural infill to the original contours and texture of each beam (PSX Summer 2018).

Late 2017: Ravaged beams (Luke Addington).

April 2018: renovated beams and ribs east of the east tower (Bob Vint).

Morales in early 2017 presents new estimates for work on the east tower, but with completion not till November 2023 (PSX Board -19-2017). In the east tower's first floor work continues through 2017 in removing cement plaster from the walls, the deep doorways, the similarly deep south window niche, and the cross-vaulted ceiling. The Patronato decides to leave the Franciscan masonry still visible with its brickwork array atop the south niche and a glimpse into the construction of the steps.

The half dome at the east tower's south window with bricks visible under a light lime wash and steps half-restored: a view into the 1700s in contrast to the full similar renovation in the west transept and old chapter room (Chuck Albanese).

First floor work focuses on beam pockets to securely anchor the newly renovated beams while avoiding direct contact with the mud adobe walls and termites likely inside the walls. At the east wall east of the tower, old plaster removal shows that the room was once twice as large. At some point the room was divided almost in half by a new adobe wall, but with no connection to the walls it abutted to the north and south. To keep the wall in place and minimize seismic risk, thick steel straps are anchored into a wood beam above the wall and drop to where its top courses of adobe are removed to embed the steel into a concrete bond beam poured on top of the wall.

By June 2017, Vince Morales is pursuing a career as a real estate agent after years as the key assistant to his dad, Danny Morales. Grandfather Sonny moves toward retiring after 65 years at San Xavier. And estimates as to when work on the east tower with a full crew can finally begin keep fading into the future. In June and July 2018, Danny decides to depart, removing his scaffolding and other equipment from the construction yard west of the mission. For the first time since the 1940s, the Morales family is no longer working on or directing renovation at San Xavier (R. Vint 6-21-2017).

Danny's decision to work elsewhere and attempts to persuade him to reconsider leave most of a long list of needs on hold, but on other fronts the Patronato is able to recruit new help:

• Kimberly Ely joins the Patronato in July as director of fundraising and marketing. She had been a vice president for development for the Tucson Symphony since moving to Tucson in 2016, and has a degree in art history plus a Thunderbird School MBA.

• Starr Herr-Cardillo is named coordinator of an update of the 1998 conservation master plan. A University of Arizona geography graduate, she earned a UA certificate in heritage conservation, and is studying conservation at the University of Pennsylvania. Job 1: Create an accessible data base of all San Xavier materials. Job 2: Direct new assessments of all the structures.

• At the mission, the Patronato assumes responsibility for the museum in the old chapter room, the east tower, and the two adobe rooms west of the entry to the south arcade and courtyard. Patronato director and UA Prof. Nancy Odegaard, a conservator at the Arizona State Museum, directs apprentices, ASM staff, and volunteers in conserving the exhibits, repairing display cases, and preparing new lightweight wall displays.

In October, Eric Means, an historic renovation contractor at the Empire Ranch, Fort Huachuca, Hotel Congress, and other sites, begins work on three small projects, then in the spring works on repairing delaminated roof plaster and patching cracks by size with ties to solid lower plaster, flexible infill caulking, marble dust, and the traditional lime wash with juice from the prickly pear. The Patronato agrees to experiment with an array of treatments above the old chapter room, tracked area by area to see over time what works best. In June 2019 Means turns to caulking gaps up to $1/4$-inch wide behind the mesquite nosing atop the risers and fronting the treads on the exterior plaster steps up the west tower. On some treads the mesquite is sanded so water will drain.

In November 2018, the National Fund for Sacred Places announces that the Patronato on behalf of the San Xavier Parish is one of 13 more congregations and non-profits to receive up to $250,000. The Philadelphia-based partner of the National Trust for Historic Preservation was launched in 2016 with $14 million from the Lilly Endowment and received 178 applications for the 2018-2019 awards (PSX Winter 2018).

In early 2019, scaffolding is erected in the top half of the west transept. Access to the *Santo* in his wood coffin is mostly unimpeded. Scaffolding to the left and right supports two tiers of metal decking up above. Rubio and Lewis direct cleaning and maintenance of the upper walls and vault for the first time since 1993. It's soon evident that an interval of over a quarter century is way too long to wait, but no one wants continual scaffolding. A possible solution would be acquisition of a hi-tech mobile lift as used at the Vatican at night. Several conservators can be hoisted to the top of the Sistine Chapel on a cantilevered, multi-hinged crane that by day is compact and wheeled out of sight.

Four of the 315 plaster stars about an inch across in the top of the west transept. These are the survivors of probably more than a thousand such stars before the ravages of leaks, heat, and tremors (David Carter).

Santa Teresa in 26 years of dust and lint but wearing her biretta as a Doctor of the Church (Tohono Restoration).

In a corner near the top of the west transept is a dove's nest of twigs and down with a single small egg, intact but long abandoned. All of the cornices and saints are shrouded in dust, especially Santa Teresa de Ávila in the medallion in the top center. She holds an open book symbolic of her notable writings, but the almost flat pages are covered in nearly an inch of dust, lint, and bits of hair. Less dusty under the top of the medallion is her black and silver beretta indicative of a saint among saints: a Doctor of the Church. That was the status recognized here by the Franciscans of the 1790s but not by the Vatican till 1970, when Pope Paul VI proclaimed her the first woman so honored.

Friends of Western Art raises $50,000 for the Patronato at a live auction on Oct. 12 at the Mountain Oyster Club. Twenty-five artists produce and donate paintings for the auction, many of them depicting the mission.

In the first weeks of March 2020, everyone at Mass is encouraged to wear a bandana, scarf, or dust mask. Gloves or no holding hands is advised during the Lord's Prayer and no embraces or handshakes as best wishes for peace unto others. Trying to maintain distancing in a compact setting is difficult, but the main challenge is limited ventilation and no air-conditioning.

2019 eve of the feast day of San Xavier: a golden reliquary with tiny remains of bone from the saint is on display for the first time in over 60 years. The authenticity of the relic is confirmed in a 1934 certificate in Latin signed by the bishop of Caserta north of Naples (Matilde Rubio).

Conservator intern Susie Moreno explains cleaning & stabilization of the San Francisco to Fr. Bill Minkel, pastor since Sept. 1, 2019. The first Francisco is now back in the upper west transept (David Carter).

On Sept. 1, 2019, Pastor Barnufksy steps down after 16½ years, the second-longest service in the mission's history: exceeded only by Fr. J. B. Llorens from 1790 to 1815. In 2003, says Barnufksy, he had no idea that most of his tenure would be as the pastor of a job site. He is succeeded by Fr. Bill Minkel, who in the preceding seven years based in Covered Wells ministered to villages on the western districts of the Tohono O'odham Nation. Till 1997 he was a San Francisco police officer for 19 years, including time as the chauffeur for the mayor. Today he says he is still hearing confessions, but no longer has to read anyone their Miranda rights. Since 2016 he has served as one of six friars on the Definitorium – assistants to the provincial minister for the Franciscans in Arizona and California.

2020: Covid-19 disruptions on, off, and on

Docent tours are suspended indefinitely on March 12. Masses are suspended on March 14, and the church is closed for almost 3 months. Except once for First Communions, Masses are not resumed for 21 weeks – till Aug. 8, but even then only in the courtyard for no more than 25 worshipers per service. In the interior

2020 virtual Christmas concert with soloist Lindsey McHugh recording in early July (Kimberly Ely).

from June 2020, Pastor Minkel re-opens the church but reduces the usual 10 hours it's open every day of the year to 3 hours a day and later 5 hours. Parishioners and visitors can enter the rear 20 feet of the church for up to 5 minutes, but only a limited number at any one time. The life-size crucifix at the south wall in the *sotocoro* is moved to the center of the nave behind candle racks and cordoned off pews. The small niches for bowls of holy water are empty and sanitizer is available at the front doors and the west doors.

On the eve and feast day of San Francisco of Assisi, docents help direct hundreds into three lines: into the church and out its west door; to and from the Mortuary Chapel; and into the courtyard to a bier of the *Santo*. On Dec. 5, 2020, Saturday p.m. and all Sunday Masses are again cancelled. Late in the year the church, the Mortuary Chapel, and the gift shop are closed, reopening only in early February 2021. Masses resume on Feb. 27 but still in the courtyard except for 7:30 a.m. Mass on weekdays in the church.

An upside to the Covid restrictions is the beginning of the long-discussed plans to renovate the west doors, their hardware, and the jambs or framing set into the brick walls. Termite damage in the jambs is so extensive that too little solid wood remains to fully support the hinges. On April 20, 2020 Luke Addington moves

Covid restrictions from June 2020 into at least fall 2021 leave most of the church closed off, including access to the Santo in the west transept and the Mother of Sorrows in the east transept. The west doors in this view are away under renovation, but are re-installed in June 2021 with interior colors close to those of the painted doors at right (A.A. Kilroy).

Late 2020: Midway to cleaning on the upper south wall, west transept – yet to be cleaned to the lower right, cleaned on the upper left with the almost black untouched "witness" rectangle (see page 74) at lower left (Matilde Rubio).

the doors to his studio, but still in place are modern screened iron doors for security after hours. Over months of conservation, Addington finds that years of various oils and varnishes artificially darkened the pine while eroding its grain.

More good news in April is that 19 months of fundraising total $500,000, allowing the Patronato to secure the maximum $250,000 matching grant from the National Fund for Sacred Places.

On July 10, 2020, Padre Kino advances another step toward canonization. Pope Francis approves the July 7 recommendation of the Vatican's Congregation for Causes of Saints that Kino be declared Venerable in recognition of his "life of heroic virtue." For Kino to advance to the next step of being declared Blessed, the Vatican will need to confirm a miracle attributed to prayer for Kino's intercession. The faithful are encouraged to seek such help in time of need (Weisenburger 2020).

In February 2021, contractor Eric Means proposes basalt fiber reinforced rebar and rope as an alternative to fiberglass in east tower repair. Removal of the cement plaster on the top of the tower brings another revelation. The top layer of 1790s brick is a bit of a hodge-podge because only its outside and inside perimeters will be visible from below. Within the top is some broken brick and the specialty curving cornice bricks as used just below the exterior top of the tower and in the projecting cornices of the three lower levels (R. Vint 3-9-2021).

The Means Building crew begins working on the three upper floors of the east tower in March. They include Wa:k resident Jarvis Juan plus César Guerrero, Octavio and Carlos Aguirre from the Ímuris vicinity, Ken Gilbert, and Derrick Hack.

March 2021: A newly restored bell in the west tower as supervised by Patronato director Nancy Odegaard. The bell now hangs from new long-lasting bolts (Miles Green).

Donations to date from the Southwestern Foundation established by Jane Ivancovich total $1 million. Not far behind is the Board of Hostesses of the Silver & Turquoise Ball, the late spring gala at the Arizona Inn that has produced $780,000 for the renovations at San Xavier.

In addition, the virtual 2020 concert succeeds in attracting a wider audience beyond the tight confines of the numbers who can be present at the actual concerts, and netting considerable funding.

A shade cloth on top of the scaffolding plus misting helps maintain cooler temperatures and more humidity to promote curing of the lime mortar repairs. The inside and outside of each of the eight pillars of the upper tower have vertical cracks about 8 inches deep splitting full bricks between joints above and below. This is likely due to the lateral rocking tremors of the 1887 quake. The cracks severely impair the structural strength of the upper tower, but are repaired with basalt rebar and ties into the brick recreating monolithic pillars instead of fragmented ones.

Another issue is powdery brick and mortar on the lower courses of the top 4th-floor pillars. Nails hammered into the bricks in the 1950s to anchor cement plaster eventually rusted because of leaks.

August 2021: Eric Means applying self-leveling sealer around a ring of flexible but non-conductive basalt rebar in the top of the east tower to protect against tremors. Preparing more sealer and then an adhesive overlay: César Guerrero in the middle and Octavio Aguirre at right. The top two-thirds of the 4½" trough is later packed with lime mortar, then the entire top of the tower is covered with basalt mesh and more mortar (Bob Vint).

Moisture trapped by the cement plaster compounds the problem by eroding the brick. Each pillar is left bearing on a smaller base (all its weight supported by less masonry), but infill with new but similar brick from Querobabi, Son. plus basalt mesh in lime mortar returns the pillars to full bearing.

July 9, 2021: A lightning warning detector is installed, a loan from inventor Leon Byerly and manufacturer Thomas Sinding of Wxline for the duration of east tower repairs. The detector's horn and strobe provide alerts for lightning within 5 miles. Conductors, clamps, and lightning rods donated by Byerly provide full grounding for the scaffolding connected to the mission's existing lightning protection.

In late fall 2021, Means reports that repair of issues unknown before removal of 1950s cement plaster has caused about two months of delay, but completion of the east tower is expected in April 2022. (PSX Conservation 9-8-2021).

———————————

So it stands, a church in the desert. There have been changes, but Mission San Xavier del Bac remains as spectacularly beautiful as it has ever been. Its graceful lines blend perfectly with the sky that looks down upon the desert and upon the O'odham houses and community buildings near the church. It will continue as a place of worship for O'odham and for others and as a sight to inspire the visitor with awe long after those of us today are gone. It is a monument to humankind's timeless devotion to God.

God in the details: intricate embossing on Santo Domingo over 18 feet up in the west transept (David Carter).

June 2021: west doors back in place. A 11-week renovation ran to over 13 months, but conservator Luke Addington believes he can now work on site to clean and repair all the other door, windows, and other wood (David Carter).

The church interior

The five *retablos* or altars in the church are extraordinary for their elaborate *estípite* columns and sculptural detail: excellent examples of Mexican Ultra-Baroque. Fired brick was sculpted to shape for the columns, cornices, shells, and other ornament, mortared in place, then covered with lime plaster and a finish coat of fine gypsum. Tempera-applied pigments, all expensive, included vermilion (mercuric sulfide), Prussian blue (ferric ferrocyanide), orpiment, and deep blue smalt, all imported from Nueva España or possibly Europe. Colors that could conceivably have been obtained locally include red, yellow, and burnt ocher plus carbon black and copper resinate (Fontana 2010: 10, 20).

Nearly all of the *retablo mayor* or main altar was gilded or covered with silver leaf, then over-painted with transparent colored glazes. The artisans used stenciling in places, applied shading, and enlivened their figures – including at least 171 angels – with motion in typical baroque tradition.

Not counting the lions old or new, 49 carved statues were likely made in guild workshops in today's central Mexico and brought to San Xavier where some were vested in plaster by the mission's sculptor(s).

In addition to paintings of angels, floral elements, and individual saints, there are very large murals of the Annunciation, the Visitation, Adoration of the Shepherds, Adoration of the Magi, Our Lady of the Pillar and Santiago, Our Lady of the Rosary, the Education of the Virgin Mary, the Virgin Mary and Child, the Pentecost, the Last Supper, the Divine Shepherdess, Santa Rosa de Viterbo, Santa Rosalía de Palermo, San Francisco Solano among the Indians, San Francisco de Asís in his Fiery Chariot, Santo Dominigo Receiving the Rosary, and two of the Crucifixion. Too, everywhere there are sculptured shells symbolizing Santiago (St. James the Greater), the patron saint of Spain, as well as baptism and pilgrimage.

San Xavier's interior is by far the best preserved and most inspiring of that of any Spanish church in what today is the United States, and even among the churches of Latin America, it ranks as extraordinary.

The east angel of the crossing with San Matías in the niche below. Till the 1990s, the hands held a long wooden pole with a festive banner at Christmas and sometimes other special occasions. The longtime usage has been reluctantly discontinued because of the risk of damage (Edward McCain).

The nave, the sotocoro, the choir loft, and the south walls of the east and west transepts with the copy of an engraving based on a Murillo at top right (Edward McCain)

Mary diapering the Christ Child in the Murillo copy with its unrestored as-is black "witness" rectangle at upper left (Edward McCain).

In the sacristy at left: a dado spared 1950s "restoration." (Edward McCain).

The 1968 to 2002 altar by James Metz under the main dome and crossing in front of the sanctuary's retablo mayor (Edward McCain).

Upper center on the retablo mayor: La Inmaculada. Below: San Xavier. In both settings, high-baroque cherubs galore (Edward McCain).

San Pedro, prince of the Apostles, is at center left on the retablo mayor opposite the first great convert, San Pablo. Below, an angel (Edward McCain).

San Simón in the niche to the left of the tabernacle (Edward McCain).

1996 mesquite tabernacle by John Ronstadt within the original 1700s tabernacle (Edward McCain).

The 2002 altar & candlesticks (David Carter).

Detail: Santo Domingo receiving the Rosary from La Virgen and El Niño. Choir loft, upper west wall. Next page left: Santo Domingo in the upper north altar, west transept. (Edward McCain).

In the west transept: a medallion, above, of Santa Gertrudis la Magna and, below, Santo Domingo (1170-1221), founder of the Dominicans, with wood cross and small puppy at his feet (Edward McCain).

In the southwest corner of the choir loft: the apostle San Marco with his traditional attribute or symbol – a lion. In this case, however, the painter depicts a mountain lion or jaguar – the sort of big cat that early parishioners would have known about (Edward McCain).

The mortuary chapel

The mortuary chapel and walled cemetery southwest of the church were completed in 1796. The disastrous earthquake of May 3, 1887, destroyed most of the mud adobe walls of the cemetery, whose entry was originally on the north. No one knows how many bodies are buried in the cemetery, which late in the 1900s was converted to a cactus garden. One headstone remains (if there were ever more) – that of Nicolás Martínez, a son of Mexican land grantee José María Martínez whose lands in 1874, six years after his death, were encompassed by the San Xavier Reservation. By the 1890s the villagers at Bac had probably created a cemetery just west of the reservation boundary and then opened the present cemetery west of the mission. A 1906 marble tablet in Latin above the door of the mortuary chapel says, in translation:

THIS CHAPEL FORMERLY A MORTUARY
THE BISHOP OF TUCSON RESTORED & DEDICATED
TO THE MOST HOLY MOTHER OF SORROWS
A.D. MCMVI

A Latin inscription on the face of the chapel altar, probably also placed there early in 1906 by Bishop Granjon, reads:

HAIL GENEROUS QUEEN
THE FIRST ROSE OF MARTYRS
AND LILY OF VIRGINS

The chapel has become a popular destination for visiting pilgrims to leave their votive candles, holy pictures, statues of saints or similar offerings – including messages of thanks or petition (Fontana 1986). The cactus garden has become almost as popular as site where people leave images of departed pets.

The north altar in the west transept with angels flanking the San José brought to San Xavier from Tumacácori in 1848 (Edward McCain).

San Felipe the apostle? in the west transept, south wall at the crossing (Edward McCain).

San Pedro Regalado (1390-1456) of Valladolid. The heart represents his zeal and the flames said to have risen once from his body. West transept, upper southwest niche (Edward McCain).

Beato Bernardino de Feltro (1439-1494): Apostle and lender to the poor. East transept, upper niche between the north and east altars (Edward McCain).

San Benito de Palermo? (1526-1589): Cook, illiterate lay brother, and reluctant Franciscan superior: East transept, upper north niche (Edward McCain).

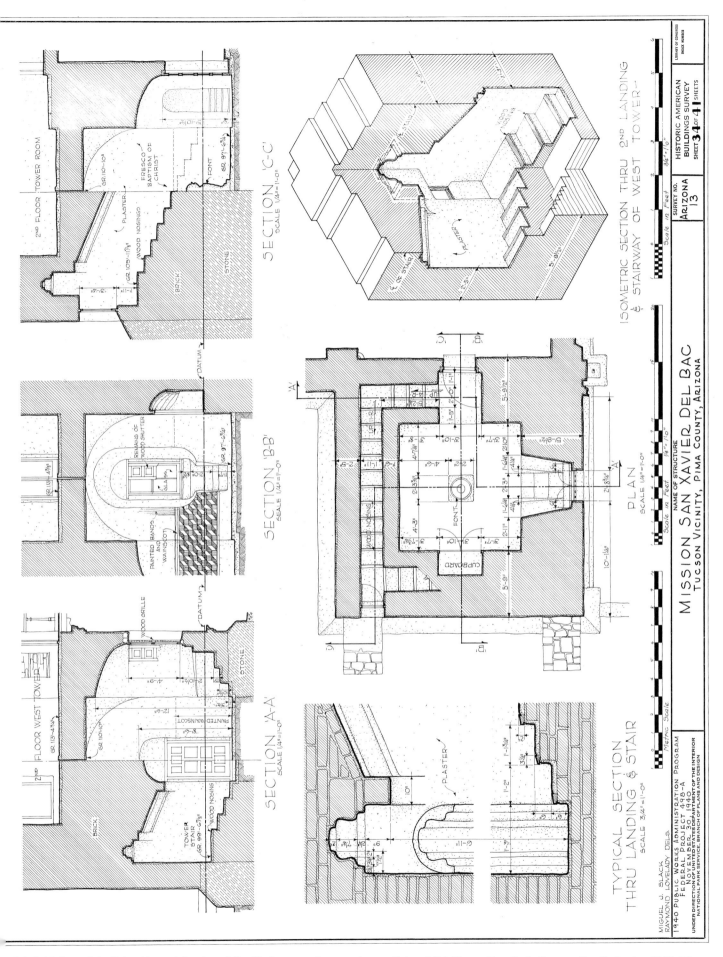

SECTION 'C-C'
SCALE 1/4"=1'-0"

2ND FLOOR TOWER ROOM

FRESCO BAPTISM OF CHRIST

PLASTER

WOOD NOSINGS

BRICK

STONE

FONT

ISOMETRIC SECTION THRU 2ND LANDING & STAIRWAY OF WEST TOWER

SECTION 'B-B'
SCALE 1/4"=1'-0"

REMAINS OF WOOD SHUTTER

GLASS

PAINTED BANDS AND WAINSCOT

SECTION 'A-A'
SCALE 1/4"=1'-0"

2ND FLOOR WEST TOWER

WOOD GRILLE

PAINTED WAINSCOT

TOWER STAIR

WOOD NOSING

BRICK

STONE

PLAN
SCALE 1/4"=1'-0"

WOOD NOSING

FONT

CUPBOARD

TYPICAL SECTION THRU LANDING & STAIR
SCALE 3/4"=1'-0"

PLASTER

MISSION SAN XAVIER DEL BAC
TUCSON VICINITY, PIMA COUNTY, ARIZONA

NAME OF STRUCTURE

SURVEY NO.
ARIZONA
13

HISTORIC AMERICAN
BUILDINGS SURVEY
SHEET 34 OF 41 SHEETS

LIBRARY OF CONGRESS
INDEX NUMBER

MIGUEL J. SLACK
RAYMOND LOVELADY DELS.

1940 PUBLIC WORKS ADMINISTRATION PROGRAM
FEDERAL PROJECT 498-A
NOVEMBER 30, 1940
UNDER DIRECTION OF UNITED STATES DEPARTMENT OF THE INTERIOR
NATIONAL PARK SERVICE, BRANCH OF PLANS AND DESIGN

et 34 of 41 sheets of detailed architectural drawings of San Xavier approved on ~~. 30, 1940 by the chief architect of the National Park Service, Thomas Vint,

the grandfather of Bob Vint, architect for the Patronato San Xavier since 1989. The drawings can be seen here: https://www.loc.gov/resource/hhh.az0061.sheet/?sp=1.

*"Garan" in Japanese means temple. "Dioz" is a variant of "Dios,"
the Spanish word for God. The unusual lettering is above the door of the
tabernacle, the temple of God to Catholics. Construction here ended in
1797, the 200th anniversary of the crucifixion at Nagasaki, Japan, of 26
Franciscans and Jesuits, most of them Japanese or Korean, to try to eradicate
Christianity. The Franciscans here were likely well aware of the anniversary,
and perhaps had a Latin-Japanese missal (David Carter).*

Tim Lewis over 30 feet up in the west transept repairing a crack (David Carter).

References

Ahlborn, Richard E.
1974   *The Sculpted Saints of a Borderland Mission: Los Bultos de San Xavier
        del Bac.* Tucson: Southwestern Mission Research Center.

Aldrich, Lorenzo D.
1950   *A Journal of the Overland Route to California & The Gold Mines.*
        Los Angeles: Dawson 's Book Shop.

Almada, Francisco R.
1983   *Diccionario de historia, geografía, y biografía sonorenses.* Hermosillo:
        Gobierno del Estado de Sonora.

Anonymous
n.d.*a*   "Bosco, Rev. Aloysius (Louis) Maria." Three-page typescript,
        biographical information on Fr. Aloysius Bosco, S.J. Copy on
        file in the Archives of the Diocese of Tucson.
n.d.*b*   "Messea, Rev. Carolus (Carlos) Evasius." Four-page typescript,
        biographical information on Fr. Carlos Evasius Messea, S.J. Copy
        on file in the Archives of the Diocese of Tucson.
1930   Last of Sobaipuri Tribe [buried?] ... with 'Red Evening;' ... Left
        To White Man. *The Tucson Daily Citizen* March 14: 3.
        Tucson: Citizen Publishing Co.
1930   Last of Sobaipuri Indians dies here. *The Arizona Daily Star*
        March 15: 2. Tucson: State Consolidated Publishing Co.
1931   Indian Tribe Vanishes As Last Living Member Dies:
        Sobaipuris Once Ruled Tucson Area: Encarnacion Mamake
        Taken By Death. *The Tucson Daily Citizen* Dec. 21: 2. Tucson:
        Citizen Publishing Co.
1931   Last of Sobaipuri Tribe dies at 106. *The Arizona Daily Star*
        Dec. 22: 3. Tucson: State Consolidated Publishing Co.
1993   *One Hundred Saints: Their Lives & Likenesses Drawn from
        "Butler's Lives of the Saints" and Great Works of Western Art.*
        Boston: Little, Brown.

Astrain, Antonio
2003   St. Francis Xavier. *The Catholic Encyclopedia* 6. New York:
        Robert Appleton. Online version of the 1909 edition:
        http://new-advent.org/cathen/06233b.htm.

Baldonado, Luis, O.F.M., *editor* and *translator*
1959   Missions San José de Tumacácori and San Xavier del Ba
        in 1774. *The Kiva* 24 (April): 21-24. Tucson: Arizon
        Archaeological & Historical Society.

Barbastro, Francisco A., O.F.M.
1971   *Sonora hacia fines del siglo XVIII: Un informe del misionero franciscal
        Fray Francisco Antonio Barbastro, con otros documentos complementario
        [Documentación Histórica Mexicana 3].* Edited and annotated b
        Lino Gómez Canedo. Guadalajara: Librería Font, S.A.

Bartlett, John R.
1854   *Personal Narrative of Explorations and Incidents in Texas, New Mexic
        California, Sonora, and Chihuahua, connected with the United States an
        Mexican Boundary Commission during the years 1850, '51, '52, an
        '53.* Two volumes. New York: D. Appleton & Co. [Reprinte
        1965 – Chicago: Rio Grande Press.]

Beeching, R.
1849   [Unpublished journal by a '49er of his trek to Californi
        via San Xavier.] San Marino, CA: Huntington Library.

Bell, James G.
1932   A Log of the Texas-California Cattle Trail, 1854. Edited b
        J. Evetts Haley. *Southwestern Historical Quarterly* 35, no. 4
        290-316. Austin: Texas State Historical Assn.

Berger, J.M.
1895   Report to J. Roe Young, U.S. Indian Agent. *Annual Report of th
        Commissioner of Indian Affairs*: 108-111. Washington: Governmen
        Printing Office.
1897   Report to H.J. Cleveland, U.S. Indian Agent. *Annual Report o
        the Commissioner of Indian Affairs*: 109-110. Washington: GPO.
1899   Report to Elwood Hadley, U.S. Indian Agent. *Annual Report o
        the Commissioner of Indian Affairs*: 164-166. Washington: GPO.
1900   Report to Elwood Hadley, U.S. Indian Agent. *Annual Report o
        the Commissioner of Indian Affairs*: 199-200. Washington: GPO.

.902   Report to Elwood Hadley, U.S. Indian Agent. *Annual Report of the Commissioner of Indian Affairs*: 188-190. Washington: GPO.

.903   Report to the Commissioner of Indian Affairs. *Annual Report of the Commissioner of Indian Affairs*: 167-169. Washington: GPO.

.905   Report to the Commissioner of Indian Affairs. *Annual Report of the Commissioner of Indian Affairs*: 148-150. Washington: GPO.

Bouhours, Dominique, S.J.
.979   *The Life of St. Francis Xavier 1688* in *The Works of John Dryden* 19, Berkeley: University of California Press.

Bolton, Herbert E.
.936   *The Rim of Christendom: A Biography of Eusebio Francisco Kino, Pacific Coast Pioneer.* New York: Macmillan.

Bosco, Aloysius M., S.J.
.862   [Letter to J. B. Lamy, Bishop of Santa Fe, datelined Santa Clara (CA), Aug. 18, 1862.] Photocopies of holograph original in Spanish, typescript copy in Spanish, and typescript of English translation by Fred McAninch on file with Bernard L. Fontana, Tucson.

Brasher, Nugent
.007   The Chichilticale Camp of Francisco Vázquez de Coronado: The Search for the Red House. *New Mexico Historical Review* 82 (Fall): 433-468. Albuquerque: University of New Mexico.

Bringas de Manzaneda, Diego de
.977   *Friar Bringas Reports to the King: Methods of Indoctrination of the Frontier of New Spain, 1796-97.* Translated and edited by Daniel S. Matson and Bernard L. Fontana. Tucson: University of Arizona Press.

Brophy, Frank C.
.970   The Mystery of San Xavier del Bac. *Arizona Highways* 46 (March): 20-35. Phoenix: Arizona Highway Dept.

Browne, J. Ross
.974   *Adventures in the Apache Country. A Tour through Arizona and Sonora, 1864.* Re-edition, with introduction, annotation, and index by Donald M. Powell. Tucson: University of Arizona Press.

Burrus, Ernest J., S.J.
.961   *Kino's Plan for the Development of Pimería Alta, Arizona, and Upper California.* Tucson: Arizona Pioneers' Historical Society.

.971   *Kino and Manje: Explorers of Sonora and Arizona: Their Vision of the Future.* Rome and St. Louis: Jesuit Historical Institute.

Cammack, Alberta, C.S.J.
.990   Religious Women at San Xavier del Bac. *Dove of the Desert* 5 (Spring): 2-3. Tucson: Friends of San Xavier Mission.

Caywood, Louis R.
.935   Bodies of Franciscan Priests Reburied. *Southwestern Monuments Monthly Report*, supplement for February 1935: 91-93. N.p.: Dept. of the Interior, National Park Service, Southwestern Monuments.

Chamberlain, Samuel E.
.956   A Lost Love and a New Adventure, *Life* 41, part 1, no. 6: 64-83. Chicago: Time Inc.

Cheek, Annetta L.
.974   "The Evidence for Acculturation in Artifacts: Indians and Non-Indians at San Xavier del Bac, Arizona." Unpublished Ph.D. dissertation, University of Arizona, Tucson.

Clark, Jeff
.020   Life of the Gila: Salado – Bringing Worlds Together. *https://www.archaeologysouthwest.org/2020/03/19/*

Clarke, A.B.
.852   *Travels in Mexico and California.* Boston: Wright & Hasty's Steam Press.

Coday, Dennis
.013   Dates set for St. Francis Xavier exposition, *National Catholic Reporter,* Oct. 25. Kansas City: The NCR Publishing Co.

Cooke, Philip St. George
1848   Report of Lt. Col. P. St. George Cooke of his March from Santa Fe, New Mexico, to San Diego, Upper California. *House Executive Documents*, no. 41, 30th Congress, 1st session: 551-563. Washington: Wendell & Van Benthuysen.

Couts, Cave J.
1961   *Hepah, California! The Journal of Cave Johnson Couts from Monterrey, Nuevo León, Mexico to Los Angeles, California during the Years 1848-1849.* Edited by Henry F. Dobyns. Tucson: Arizona Pioneers' Historical Society.

Cox, Cornelius C.
1925   From Texas to California in 1849, edited by Maybelle E. Martin. *Southwestern Historical Quarterly* 29, no. 2: 128-46, Austin: Texas State Historical Assn.

Crosby, Anthony
2008   "Trip Report, San Xavier del Bac, Tucson, AZ, Feb. 15, 2008." 17 pp. Unpublished typescript, copy on file with the Patronato San Xavier, Tucson.

Densmore, Frances
1929   *Papago Music* [Smithsonian Institution, Bureau of American Ethnology, Bulletin 90]. Washington: GPO.

Diehl, Michael W.
2018   Foraging and Farming. *Archaeology Southwest Magazine* 32 (Fall): 16-17. Tucson: Archaeology Southwest.

Dobyns, Henry F.
1959   Some Spanish Pioneers in Upper Pimería. *The Kiva* 25 (October): 18-21. Tucson: Arizona Archaeological & Historical Society.

1960   "The Priests of Bac." Unpublished manuscript, copy on file in Special Collections MS 461, University of Arizona Library, Tucson.

1976   *Spanish Colonial Tucson: A Demographic History.* Tucson: University of Arizona Press.

Doelle, William H.
2018a   Tucson Underground. *Archaeology Southwest Magazine* 32 (Fall): 3-5. Tucson: Archaeology Southwest.

2018b   Preserving Tucson's Ballcourt Villages. *Archaeology Southwest Magazine* 32 (Fall): 24-25. Tucson: Archaeology Southwest.

Doelle, William H. and J. Homer Thiel
2018   Greater Tucson's Hohokam Villages, AD 500-1150. *Archaeology Southwest Magazine* 32 (Fall): 21-22. Tucson: Archaeology Southwest.

Doelle, William H., Henry D. Wallace, and J. Homer Thiel
2018   Greater Tucson's Hohokam Villages, AD 1150-1450. *Archaeology Southwest Magazine* 32 (Fall): 28-29. Tucson: Archaeology Southwest.

Donohue, J. Augustine, S.J.
1960   The Unlucky Jesuit Mission of Bac, 1732-1767. *Arizona and the West*, 2 (Summer): 127-139. Tucson: University of Arizona Press.

1969   *After Kino: Jesuit Missions in Northwestern New Spain, 1711-1767 [Sources & Studies for the History of the Americas* 6]. Rome and St. Louis: Jesuit Historical Institute.

Downum, Christian E., Paul R. Fish, and Suzanne K. Fish
2009   Refining the Role of Cerros de Trincheras in Southern Arizona Settlement. *The Kiva* 75 (Winter): 261-287. Tucson: Arizona Archaeological & Historical Society.

Drexel, Mother Katharine, S.B.S.
1894   *Original Annals.* Bensalem, PA: Sisters of the Blessed Sacrament

1905   *Journal of Promises* (WMMK #3203). Unpublished typescript with annotated corrections and records of payments fulfilled. Bensalem, PA: Sisters of the Blessed Sacrament.

Duarte, Carmen
1986   O'odham Constitution unites old and new. *The Arizona Daily Star*: March 9: 1D. Tucson: Star Publishing Co.

DuBois, Susan M., and Ann W. Smith
1980   The 1887 Earthquake in San Bernardino Valley, Sonora: Historic Accounts and Intensity Patterns in Arizona. *Special Paper*, no. 3. Tucson: State of Arizona, Bureau of Geology & Mineral Technology, University of Arizona.

Duffen, William A., *editor*
1960   Overland via "Jackass Mail" in 1858, the Diary of Phocian R. Way. *Arizona and the West* 2 (Summer): 147-64. Tucson: University of Arizona Press.

Duffy, Consuela Marie, S.B.S.
1966   *Katharine Drexel: A Biography.* Philadelphia: The Peter Reilly Co.

Duffy, Mary Aquinas, C.S.J.
n.d.   [Letter to Rt. Rev. Daniel J. Gercke, Bishop of Tucson.] Unpublished letter ca. 1924. Copy on file with Bernard L. Fontana, Tucson.

Dunne, Peter M., S.J.
1941   Capt. Anza and the Case of Fr. Campos. *Mid-America* 23 (January): 45-60. Chicago: Loyola University.
1957   *Juan Antonio Balthasar, Padre Visitador to the Sonora Frontier: 1744-1745.* Two original reports. Tucson: Arizona Pioneers' Historical Society.

Durivage, John E.
1937   Through Mexico to California: Letters & Journals of John E. Durivage, *Southwest Historical Series* 5, edited by Ralph P. Bieber: 159-225. Glendale: The Arthur H. Clark Co.

Eccleston, Robert
1950   *Overland to California on the Southwestern Trail: 1849.* Edited by George P. Hammond and Edward Howes. Berkeley & Los Angeles: University of California Press.

Emory, William H.
1857   *Report on the United States & Mexican Boundary Survey Made Under the Direction of the Secretary of the Interior by William H. Emory, Major First Cavalry, and U.S. Commissioner.* Two volumes. Washington: A.O.P. Nicholson, Printer.

Engelhardt, Zephyrin, O.F.M.
1899   *The Franciscans in Arizona.* Harbor Springs, MI: Holy Childhood Indian School.

Evans, George W.
1945   *Mexican Gold Trail: The Journal of a Forty-Niner.* Edited by Glenn S. Dumke. San Marino, CA: Huntington Library.

Farmer, David H.
1992   *The Oxford Dictionary of Saints 3.* Oxford: Oxford University Press.

Faulk, Odie
1966   Introduction. In *John Baptiste Salpointe. Soldier of the Cross*, edited by Odie B. Faulk, pp. ix-xix. Tucson: Diocese of Tucson.

Fontana, Bernard L.
1970   "A History of the Legal Status of Land and of Land Use on the San Xavier Indian Reservation, Arizona." 30 pp. Unpublished typescript, copy on file with Bernard L. Fontana, Tucson.
1973   "Excavations at San Xavier: Field Notes May 2, 1962 - Feb. 17, 1973." 170 pp. Unpublished notes and typescript. Archives A-643, Arizona State Museum, Tucson.
1976   *The Papago Indians.* Sells, Arizona: Title IV-A, Indian Education Act, Indian Oasis Schools.
1986   Pilgrimage to San Xavier. *Arizona Highways* 62 (November): 44-48. Phoenix: Arizona Dept. of Transportation.
1987   Santa Ana de Cuiquiburitac: Pimería Alta's Northernmost Mission. *Journal of the Southwest* 29 (Summer): 133-159. Tucson: University of Arizona Press & The Southwest Center.
1993a   Saving San Xavier: The Role of a Patronato. In *The Spanish Missionary Heritage of the United States. Selected Papers and Commentaries from the November 1990 Quincentenary Symposium*, edited by Howard Benoist and María Carolina Flores: 230-237.

San Antonio, TX: U.S. Dept. of the Interior/National Park Service & Los Compadres de San Antonio Missions National Historical Park.
1993b   Conservation work at Mission San Xavier del Bac #21. *Mass bulletin* April 25: 2. Bac: San Xavier Parish
1994   *Entrada: The Legacy of Spain and Mexico in the United States.* Tucson: Southwest Parks & Monuments Assn.
1995   Restoring San Xavier del Bac, "Our Church:" Tohono O'odham Work to Restore the 200-Year-Old Church Built by Their Ancestors. *Native Peoples* 8 (Summer): 28-35. Phoenix: Media Concepts Group Inc.
1996a   Who Were the Decorators and Builders of Mission San Xavier del Bac? *The Kiva* 61 (Summer): 365-384. Tucson: Arizona Archaeological & Historical Society.
1996b   The O'odham. *The Pimería Alta: Missions & More*: 19-27. Tucson: The Southwestern Mission Research Center
2010   *A Gift of Angels: The Art of Mission San Xavier del Bac* with photographs by Edward McCain & diagrams by Bob Vint. Tucson: University of Arizona Press.

Forbes, Jack D.
1965   *Warriors of the Colorado: The Yumans of the Quechan Nation and Their Neighbors.* Norman: University of Oklahoma Press.

Foster, Nancy L.
1969   "The Restoration and Preservation of Mission San Xavier del Bac, 1940-1969." 23 pp. Unpublished typescript term paper for Anthropology 294, University of Arizona. Copy on file in Special Collections, University of Arizona Library, Tucson.

Fox, Francis J., S.J.
1974   Laying the Foundations for the Diocese of Tucson: The Coming of Salpointe, 1866. *The Smoke Signal* 30 (Fall): 257-264. Tucson: Tucson Corral of the Westerners.

Froebel, Julius
1859   *Seven Years' Travel in Central America, Northern Mexico, and the Far West of the United States.* London: Richard Bentley.

Gabel, Norman
1931   "Martinez Hill Ruins: An Example of Prehistoric Culture of the Middle Gila." Unpublished M.A. thesis, University of Arizona, Tucson.

Garate, Donald
n.d.   "Juan Bauptista de Belderrain Igarza." Unpublished two-page typescript on the grandparents, parents, and siblings of Juan Bautista Velderrain from the Libro de Bautizados en la Parrochial de Cizurquil, Spain. Copy on file with Bernard L. Fontana, Tucson.

Garcés, Francisco Hermenegildo, O.F.M.
1900   *On the Trail of a Spanish Pioneer: The Diary and Itinerary of Francisco Garcés in His Travels through Sonora, Arizona, and California, 1775-1776.* Elliott Coues, translator and editor. Two volumes. New York: Francis P. Harper.

Geiger, Maynard, O.F.M.
1939   *The Kingdom of St. Francis in Arizona (1539-1939).* Santa Barbara, CA: N.p.
1953   A Voice from San Xavier del Bac (1802-1805). *Provincial Annals* Vol. 16, no. 1, pp. 5-11. Santa Barbara: Santa Barbara Province of the Order of Friars Minor.

Giffords, Gloria F.
1978   Untitled study describing the statues of Mission Tumacácori. MS copy on file at Tumacácori National Historical Park.
1990   Spanish Colonial Polychrome Statuary: Replicating the Lions of San Xavier del Bac. *APT Bulletin* 22, no. 3: 19-25. Champagne, IL: Assn. for Preservation Technology.

Giffords, Gloria F., and Miguel Celorio
1985   "Report on the Condition of the Interior of Mission San Xavier del Bac, Tucson, Arizona." 50 pp. Unpublished typescript. Copy on file with Bob Vint, Tucson.

Granjon, Henry, D.D.
1911   [Letter written at Tucson, May 30, 1911.] Photocopy on file with Bernard L. Fontana, Tucson.

Gray, Andrew B.

1852   [Letter to John R. Bartlett, Commissioner, U.S. Boundary Survey.] *Senate Executive Documents* 119, 32nd Congress, 1st session, vol. 14: 267-269. Washington.

Grijalva, Andrés

1768   "Inventory of what was entrusted to the ministers of Sonora, year of 1768." Translated by Jorge Olvera. Copy on file with Bernard L. Fontana, Tucson. [The Spanish original is in "Inventarios de lo que se entrego a los Ministros de Sonora, año de 1768", Archivo del Colegio de la Santa Cruz de Querétaro, K. Núm. 8, legajo 14.]

Hall, Dawn, editor

1996   *Drawing the Borderline: Artist-Explorers of the U.S.-Mexico Boundary Survey.* Albuquerque: Albuquerque Museum.

Hammond, George P.

1929   Primería [*sic*] Alta after Kino's Time. *New Mexico Historical Review* 4 (July): 220-238. Santa Fe: Historical Society of New Mexico.

Hayes, Benjamin

1929   *Pioneer Notes from the Diaries of Judge Benjamin Hayes, 1849-1875.* Edited by Marjorie T. Wolcott. Los Angeles: privately printed.

Herreras, Eleazar D.

1981   "A Report of the Restoration and Preservation of San Xavier del Bac,Tucson, Arizona, to the American Institute of Architects, Committee on Preservation of Historic Buildings, Washington, D.C." 25 pp. plus appendices and photographs. Unpublished typescript. Bac: San Xavier Parish.

Herrick, Hannah M. and Christopher H. Baisan

2019   Dendrochronology at the Mission San Xavier del Bac convento (Tucson, Arizona, USA). *Journal of Archaeological Science:* Reports 25: 40-46. *www.elsevier.com/locate/jasrep*

Hine, Robert V.

1968   *Bartlett's West: Drawing the Mexican Boundary.* New Haven and London: Yale University Press.

Holben, Randon E., and Leland L. Lawrence

1985   "Preliminary Study of the Structural Condition of Mission San Xavier del Bac." 21 pp. & appendices. Unpublished typescript. Copy on file with the Patronato San Xavier, Tucson in Section 2, *Conservation Master Plan: Mission San Xavier del Bac,* a Patronato submittal on March 10, 1997 to the Getty Grant Program.

Holterman, Jack

1973   "God's Vagabond: An Interpretation of Francisco Garcés." Unpublished typescript, copy on file with David Carter, Tucson.

Horgan, Paul

1975   *Lamy of Santa Fe: His Life and Times.* New York: Farrar, Straus & Giroux.

Hosmer, John, and others, *editors*

1991   From the Santa Cruz to the Gila in 1850. An Excerpt from the Journal of William P. Huff. *Journal of Arizona History* 32 (Spring): 41-110. Tucson: Arizona Historical Society.

Howlett, W.J.

1908   *Life of the Right Reverend Joseph P. Machebeuf, D.D.* Pueblo, CO: Franklin Press Co. [Reprint 1987 – Denver: Regis College with a foreword, endnotes, and index by Thomas J. Steele, S.J., and Ronald S. Brockway.]

Hunter, William W.

1992   *Missouri '49er. The Journal of William W. Hunter on the Southern Gold Trail.* Edited and annotated by David P. Robrock. Albuquerque: University of New Mexico Press.

Iturralde, Francisco, O.F.M.

1795   [Letter to Friar Diego Bringas, written from Tubutama, Dec. 12, 1795.] Unpublished. Microfilm copy on file in the University of Arizona Library, Tucson.

1797   "*Visita* de las Misiones de la Pimería por el P. Iturralde, Presid. te. Tubutama." Transalated by Fr. Luis Baldonado, O.F.M. Unpublished manuscript. The original is in section 9, Franciscan General Archives, Rome.

Ives, Ronald L.

1961   The Quest of the Blue Shells. *Arizoniana* 2, no. 1: 3-7. Tucson: Arizona Pioneers' Historical Society.

Jackson, Robert H.

1994   *Indian Population Decline: The Missions of Northwestern New Spain, 1687-1840.* Albuquerque: University of New Mexico Press.

Jones, Jeffrey T., Ellen C. Ruble, and William H. Doelle

2018   Zanardelli Site. *Archaeology Southwest Magazine* 32 (Fall): 29. Tucson: Archaeology Southwest.

Kessell, John L.

1966   Peaceful Conquest in Southern Arizona in *Father Kino in Arizona* 53-95. Phoenix: Arizona Historical Foundation.

1970   *Mission of Sorrows: Jesuit Guevavi and the Pimas 1691-1767.* Tucson: University of Arizona Press.

1976   *Friars, Soldiers, and Reformers: Hispanic Arizona and the Sonora Mission Frontier, 1767-1856.* Tucson: University of Arizona Press.

Kino, Eusebio Francisco, S.J.

1948   *Kino's Historical Memoir of Pimería Alta.* Translated and edited by Herbert E. Bolton. Two volumes in one. Berkeley & Los Angeles: University of California Press.

1966   Relación Diaria [1698]. Translated by Fay Jackson Smith in *Father Kino in Arizona* 8-34. Phoenix: Arizona Historical Foundation

1991   *A Kino Keepsake. Facsimile of an Original Eusebio Francisco Kino Field Diary Preserved at the University of Arizona Library, Describing Southern Arizona in 1699.* Translated with an introduction by Kieran R. McCarty and Lilián Zaragoza. Tucson: Friends of the University of Arizona Library.

Leighton, David

2014   Street Smarts: Generous nun the namesake for Drexel Road. *Arizona Daily Star:* March 4: A2, A6. Tucson: Star Publishing Co.

Ludlam, A.B.

1880   [Letter to the Commissioner of Indian Affairs, Dec. 3, 1880.] Unpublished letter on file in Record Group 75, National Archives, Washington. Typescript on file with Bernard L. Fontana, Tucson.

Manje, Juan Mateo

1954   *Luz de Tierra Incógnita: Unknown Arizona and Sonora, 1693-1701.* Translated by Harry J. Karns & Associates. Tucson: Arizona Silhouettes.

1997   *A Frontier Documentary: Sonora and Tucson 1821-1848.* Tucson: University of Arizona Press. *From an official transmission of the original May 11, 1841 report on four folios in the Archivo Histórico del Estado de Sonora, cabinet 8, drawer 1, folder 121.*

Martin, Douglas D.

1954   *Yuma Crossing.* Albuquerque: University of New Mexico Press.

Martín Bernal, Lt. Cristóbal

1966   Diary [1697]. Translated by Fay Jackson Smith in *Father Kino in Arizona* 35-47. Phoenix: Arizona Historical Foundation.

Martínez, José María, and anonymous

1858   [Report to Fr. Joseph P. Machebeuf on church property in the Santa Cruz Valley, datelined San Xavier del Bac, Dec. 16, 1858.] Holograph manuscript in the Archives of the Diocese of Tucson. Typescript copy and English translation by Kieran R. McCarty on file with Bernard L. Fontana, Tucson.

McCarty, Kieran R., O.F.M.

1975   The Colorado Massacre of 1781: María Monticello's Report. *The Journal of Arizona History* 16 (Autumn): 221-225. Tucson: Arizona Historical Society.

1976   *Desert Documentary: The Spanish Years, 1767-1821* [Historical Monograph 4]. Tucson: Arizona Historical Society.

1977a   Iturralde: 1797. In *Bac: Where the Waters Gather*, by John P. Schaefer, Celestine Chinn, O.F.M., and Kieran R. McCarty, O.F.M.: 45-47. [Tucson]: privately printed.

1977b   Zúñiga: 1804. In *Bac: Where the Waters Gather*, by John P. Schaefer, Celestine Chinn, and Kieran R. McCarty: 48-49. [Tucson]: privately printed.

1981   *A Spanish Frontier in the Enlightened Age: Franciscan Beginnings in Sonora and Arizona, 1767-1770.* Washington: Academy of American Franciscan History.
1997   *A Frontier Documentary: Sonora and Tucson, 1821-1848.* Tucson: University of Arizona Press.

McMahon, [Sister] Thomas Marie, C.S.J.
1952   "The Sisters of St. Joseph of Carondelet: Arizona's Pioneer Religious Congregation." Unpublished master's thesis, St. Louis: St. Louis University.

Michler, Nathaniel
1857   From the 111th Meridian of Longitude to the Pacific Ocean. In *Report on the United States and Mexican Boundary Survey*, by William H. Emory, *Senate Executive Documents*, no. 108, 34th Congress, 1st session, Vol. 1: 103-125. Washington: Nicholson. [Reprinted 1987 with a new introduction by William H. Goetzmann: Austin: Texas State Historical Assn.]

Miller, Joseph, editor
1962   *Arizona Cavalcade: The Turbulent Times.* New York: Hastings House.

Moore, Yndia S.
1980   Arizona Album. Eighty-five Years Ago in the Old Pueblo: Repairing San Xavier. *Tucson Citizen*, May 22: A15. Tucson: Citizen Publishing Co.

Morlock, Blake
2002   San Xavier desecration one year later. *Tucson Citizen*: Feb. 12: 1A-2A. Tucson: Citizen Publishing Co.

Morris, Stephanie
2014   "Re: St. Katharine and Mission San Xavier del Bac, Tucson". Emails: copies on file with the editor, Tucson.

Murchison, John, and Samuel Birt
1966   Journal of the La Grange Company. *Quarterly of the Tuolumne County Historical Society* 22 (December). Sonora, CA: Tuolumne County Historical Society.

Newhall, Nancy
1954   *Mission San Xavier del Bac* with photographs by Ansel Adams and drawings by Edith Hamlin: 5-18, 20-26, 28-32, 41-42, 44-47, 49-51, 53-56, 58-68. San Francisco: 5 Associates.

Nordmeyer, Robert L.
1978a   Most Rev. Henry R. Granjon (1863-1922). In *Shepherds in the Desert*, with introductory essays by Charles W. Polzer, S.J., and Kieran R. McCarty, O.F.M. 60-75. Tucson: Diocese of Tucson.
1978b   Most Rev. Peter Bourgade (1845-1908). In *Shepherds in the Desert*, with introductory essays by Charles W. Polzer, S.J., and Kieran R. McCarty, O.F.M. 40-57. Tucson: Diocese of Tucson.

Oblasser, Bonaventure, O.F.M.
1930-31 Carnacion Tells Her Tale. *Arizona Historical Review* 3 (January): 97-98. Tucson: University of Arizona with the cooperation of the Arizona Pioneers' Historical Society.
1960   [Summary of the registers of missions San Ignacio, Soamca, and Guebavi for the Jesuit period of the Pimería Alta.] Unpublished typescript, copy on file with Bernard L. Fontana, Tucson.

Och, Joseph, S.J.
1965   *Missionary in Sonora: The Travel Reports of Joseph Och, S.J., 1755-1767.* Translated and annotated by Theodore E. Treutlein. San Francisco: California Historical Society.

Officer, James E.
1987   *Hispanic Arizona, 1536-1856.* Tucson: University of Arizona Press.

Pancoast, Charles E.
1930   *A Quaker Forty-niner.* Edited by Anna P. Hannum. Philadelphia: University of Pennsylvania Press.

Parke, John G.
1857   Report of Explorations for that Portion of a Railroad Route Near the Thirty-second Parallel of North Latitude Lying between Doña Ana, on the Río Grande, and Pimas Villages, on the Gila. *Senate Executive Documents*, no. 78, Vol. 2, 33rd Congress, 2nd session. Washington: Beverly Tucker.

Patronato San Xavier
1978   "Articles of Incorporation of Patronato San Xavier." 6 pp. Signed March 31, 1978; filed with the Arizona Corporation Commission, June 15, 1978.
2020   Minutes of the Board of Directors, 1999-2020. On file with the Patronato San Xavier.
2021   *Patronato* newsletters, 1991-2021. Reports by Bernard L. Fontana, Lorraine Drachman, Vern Lamplot, Miles Green et al. Copies on file with the Patronato San Xavier, Tucson.
2021   Conservation committee minutes & construction reports, 2014-2021. On file with the Patronato San Xavier, Tucson.

Perschl, Nicholas, O.F.M.
1959   Reminiscences of a Franciscan in Papaguería. *The Kiva* 24 (February): 1-9. Tucson: Arizona Archaeological & Historical Society.

Pima County
2015   *Official Canvas & Consolidated Elections Nov. 3, 2015.* Tucson: Pima County Elections Dept..

Polzer, Charles W., S.J.
1982   *Kino Guide II: His missions – His monuments.* Tucson: Southwestern Mission Research Center.
1998   *Kino: A Legacy: His Life, His Works, His Missions, His Monuments.* Tucson: Jesuit Fathers of Southern Arizona.

Poston, Charles O.
1865   Report of the Arizona Superintendent of Indian Affairs. In *Report of the Secretary of the Interior; Report of the Commissioner of Indian Affairs* [House Executive Documents, Vol. 5, no.1, 38th Congress, 2nd session]: 294-302. Washington: Government Printing Office.

Powell, H.M.T.
1931   *The Santa Fe Trail to California 1848-1852: The Journal and Drawings of H.M.T. Powell.* Edited by Douglas S. Watson. San Francisco: The Book Club of California.

Quiroga, Joaquín
1843   "Report to the Secretary of the Dept. of Sonora in Guaymas on Mission Temporalities in the Area of Tucson-San Xavier del Bac": English translation by Jorge Olvera. Folder 121, cabinet 8, drawer 1, Archivo Histórico del Estado de Sonora, Hermosillo. Typescript copy of the original and of Olvera's translation on file with Bernard L. Fontana, Tucson.

Regan, Margaret
2000   A Saint Among Us. *Tucson Weekly:* Oct. 5.

Reff, Daniel T.
1995   The "Predicament of Culture" and Spanish Missionary Accounts of the Tepehuan and Pueblo Revolts. *Ethnohistory* 42 (Winter): 63-90. Durham, NC: Duke University Press.

Reyes, Antonio María de los, O.F.M.,
1772   "Report on the Missions of Arizona and Sonora." Translated by Kieran R. McCarty. Unpublished manuscript, copy on file in Special Collections, University of Arizona Library, Tucson.

Robinson, William J.
1963   Excavations at San Xavier del Bac, 1958. *The Kiva* 29 (December): 35-57. Tucson: Arizona Archaeological & Historical Society.

Roca, Paul M.
1967   *Paths of the Padres through Sonora: An Illustrated History & Guide to Its Spanish Churches.* Foreword by John Francis Bannon, S.J. Tucson: Arizona Pioneers' Historical Society.

Rocha y Figueroa, Gerónimo
1780   "Diario." Harvard University Library, Cambridge, MA; Sparks Manuscript Collection, no. 98. Copy made by Antonio de Bonilla in Arizpe, Sonora, Nov. 30, 1781. San Xavier portion translated by Kieran R. McCarty, O.F.M.; copy on file with Bernard L. Fontana, Tucson.

Rohder, Regis, O.F.M.
1982   *Padre to the Pápagos: Fr. Bonaventure Oblasser.* Tucson: The Oblasser Library, San Xavier Mission.

San Agustín Cathedral
1863-78   [Abstract of baptismal registers April 25, 1863 through Dec. 28, 1878. Typescript. Copy on file with Bernard L. Fontana, Tucson.

Salpointe, Jean B., D.D.
1875   [Letter to E.P. Smith, Commissioner of Indian Affairs, datelined Papago Indian Reservation, San Xavier, Arizona, Feb. 25, 1875.] Typescript copy on file with Bernard L. Fontana, Tucson.
1880   *A Brief Sketch of the Mission of San Xavier del Bac with a Description of its Church.* San Francisco: Thomas' Steam Printing House.
1898   *Soldiers of the Cross: Notes on the Ecclesiastical History of New Mexico, Arizona, and Colorado.* Banning, CA: St. Boniface's Industrial School.

San Xavier Mission
1990   *Chronicles of San Xavier Mission.* Excerpts from 1935-1959 house notes by the superior or assistants. Selected and transcribed by Bernard L. Fontana. Copy on file with David Carter, Tucson.
2021   *http://www.sxmschool.org/index.php/about-us/history*

Schellie, Don
1968   *Vast Domain of Blood: The Story of the Camp Grant Massacre.* Los Angeles: Westernlore Press.

Sedelmayr, Jacobo, S.J.
1751a   [Letter to Fr. Provincial Juan Antonio Balthasar, written at Tubutama on Jan. 9, 1751.] Photocopy on file in Special Collections, University of Arizona Library, Tucson. Translated by Daniel S. Matson; copy on file with Bernard L. Fontana, Tucson.
1751b   [Letter to Fr. Provincial Juan Antonio Balthasar, written at Tubutama on May 21, 1751.] Photocopy on file in Special Collections, University of Arizona Library, Tucson. Translated by Daniel S. Matson; copy on file with Bernard L. Fontana, Tucson.
1751c   "Visitation of the New Province of Pimería Alta, 1751." Photocopy on file in Special Collections, University of Arizona Library, Tucson. Translated by Daniel S. Matson; copy on file with Bernard L. Fontana, Tucson.

Seymour, Deni J.
2011   Dating the Sobaípuri: A Case Study in Chronology Building and Archaeological Interpretation. *Bulletin* 67 (Sept.): 11-12. Tucson: Old Pueblo Archaeology Center.

Sheridan, Thomas E.
1986   *Los Tucsonenses: The Mexican Community in Tucson 1854-1941.* Tucson: University of Arizona Press.
1988   Kino's Unforeseen Legacy: The Material Consequences of Missionization. *The Smoke Signal* 49-50 (Spring & Fall): 149-167. Tucson: Tucson Corral of the Westerners.
1996   The Columbian Exchange. *The Pimería Alta: Missions & More:* 55-56; 58-59. Tucson: The Southwestern Mission Research Center

Socies, Bartolomé, O.F.M.
1797   [Letter to Friar Diego Bringas, Apostolic Praeses, datelined San Xavier del Bac, April 28, 1797.] Unpublished manuscript, original in the Civezza Collection, Antonianum Library, Rome. Translated by Kieran R. McCarty; copy of typescript of original and of translation on file with Bernard L. Fontana, Tucson.

Sonnichsen, C. Leland
1982   *Tucson: The Life and Times of an American City.* Norman: University of Oklahoma Press.

Soto, Martin L.
1964   "Current Restoration of Mission San Xavier del Bac, 1950-1959." 19 pp. Unpublished typescript submitted for partial credit in a history course. Copy on file in Special Collections, University of Arizona Library, Tucson.

St. Barbara Province, Order of Friars Minor
2016   St. Barbara Province Elects New Provincial Minister. ESC News Archives. *https://usfranciscans.org/category/esc/page/10*

Suchet, [Sister] Marie Euphrasia, C.S.J.
1872   "Exercises on the Papago Language. St. Xavier's Convent, A.T." Unpublished manuscript no. 629, National Anthropological Archives, Smithsonian Institution, Washington.

Thiel, J. Homer
2018a   Early Farming Settlements. *Archaeology Southwest Magazine* 32 (Fall): 11-12. Tucson: Archaeology Southwest.
2018b   Farmers with Pottery. *Archaeology Southwest Magazine* 32 (Fall): 17. Tucson: Archaeology Southwest.
2018c   All about Greater Tucson Pithouses. *Archaeology Southwest Magazine* 32 (Fall): 18-19. Tucson: Archaeology Southwest.

Tumacácori, Mission San José de
varia   "Libro de Bautismos, Libra de Casamientos, Libra de Entierros de San José de Tumacácori." Archive of the Diocese of Tucson. Copy in the Arizona Historical Society, Tucson.

Underhill, Ruth
1936   *The Autobiography of a Papago Woman.* Menasha, WI: The American Anthropological Assn., Memoir no. 46.

Villiger, Burcardo, S.J.
1864   "Estrato di Lettera del P. Burcardo Villiger, Superiore della Missione de California." Holograph copy of a letter in Italian by Fr. Villiger at Santa Clara, CA, on March 8, 1864, with quotes from a letter by Fr. Carolus Messea. Photocopy of original and typescript of English translation by Donald Weinstein on file with Bernard L. Fontana, Tucson.

Vint, James M.
2018   Las Capas: "the Layers." *Archaeology Southwest Magazine* 32 (Fall): 15. Tucson: Archaeology Southwest.

Vint, Robert W.
2011   "Progress report: site visit 2.11" pp 1-4. Copy posted at *www.patronatosanxavier.org* – *Architect Reports.*
2013   "Progress report: site visit 6.19" text with 6 photos. Copy posted at *www.patronatosanxavier.org* – *Architect Reports.*
2021   Reports on site meetings, proposed renovation, and construction drawings, 1989-2021. On file with the Patronato San Xavier, Tucson.

Wallace, Henry D.
2018   Valencia/Valencia Vieja *Archaeology Southwest Magazine* 32 (Fall): 25. Tucson: Archaeology Southwest.

Wallace, Henry D. and James P. Holmlund
1984   The Classic Period in the Tucson Basin. *The Kiva* 49 (Spring) 167-194. Tucson: Arizona Archaeological & Historical Society.

Webb, Robert H., Julio L. Betancourt, R. Roy Johnson, and Raymond M. Turner
2014   *Requiem for the Santa Cruz: An Environmental History of an Arizona River.* Tucson: University of Arizona Press.

Weisenburger, Edward J.
2020   News: Venerable Padre Kino. *mail@flocknote.com* July 13 at 9:11 a.m. Diocese of Tucson.

Whedon, J. W., Jr.
1906   "Minutes Book. The Traders' National Protective Assn." Unpublished typescript of pp. 188 and 190 of the minutes book. Copy on file with Bernard L. Fontana, Tucson.

Wilbur, Dr. Reuben A.
1872   Report of the U.S. Indian Agent for the Papagoes. *Annual Report of the Commissioner of Indian Affairs for 1872: 320-322. Washington:* GPO.

Wood, Harvey
1955   *Personal Recollections of Harvey Wood.* Pasadena, CA: privately printed.

Young, J. Roe
1896   Report to the Commissioner of Indian Affairs. *Annual Report of the Commissioner of Indian Affairs:* 121-123. Washington: Government Printing Office.

Kudos!

The Southwestern Mission Research Center will forever salute the late Dr. Bernard L. "Bunny" Fontana as noted on the front fly leaf of this edition. We also thank editor David Carter for converting the 2015 edition to a chronology, creating chapters, adding a table of contents, and compiling 65 new photos plus the 40 (see below) from Edward McCain. In this edition David provides the updates over the last seven years and has attempted to carry out Bunny's 2015 wish that the next edition have much more coverage of the O'odham. Wherever possible this has been done with excerpts from Bunny's writings.

The SMRC is similarly indebted to Edward McCain, who has generously contributed 40 of his superb photographs to this edition. Most of the photographs appear in *A Gift of Angels*, but in images up to 12 by 14 inches compared with, at best, 7¼ by 9 inches here. Most of McCain's photos date to 2002. That was within only about five years from the completion of most of the interior renovation in the 1990s, so the angels, saints, and other art appear as close to pristine as possible after more than two centuries. The photographer often worked long into the night and high atop scaffolding – hundreds of hours of work. It is a pleasure to be able to offer a sampling of that effort to a new and larger audience.

Jodie Chertudi of JLewers Design converted the draft revisions and layout from the unwieldy and garbled format of a well-known word-processing software to nimble design software suitable for actual publication. She patiently reconstructed portions of the text bedeviled by hidden glitches so the words flow fluidly, and carefully inserted the many final revisions.

Becky Wigginton of West-Press has diplomatically accepted many delays and changes over the last two years. While still at her family's Commercial Printers Inc. she ably supervised the printing of the 2015 edition of this history.

Dale S. Brenneman and Allen Dart diligently copy edited the text, then Ann Brown, Bobbie Jo Buel Carter, Debbie Kornmiller, Joe McDermott, and Maria Parham provided scrupulous final proofreading. Gracias!

Acknowledgments by Bunny Fontana

The writing of history, like history itself, stands on the shoulders of those who have preceded us. For the Spanish and Mexican periods of Bac's past I have relied most heavily on the herculean efforts of scholars Henry F. Dobyns, Donald Garate, Jack Holterman, John Kessell, Daniel S. Matson, Fr. Kieran R. McCarty, and James E. Officer as well as fathers Bonaventure Oblasser, Luis Baldonado, and Charles Polzer.

Thanks are also due to the Rev. Norman Whalen; the truly wonderful Fr. Nicholas Perschl; George Eckhart; Byron Ivancovich; Donald Bufkin; and the remarkable editor, Otis Chidester – a man who knew how to extract blood from a turnip as surely as he could drag written words from reluctant authors.

And finally, a special thanks to Jane Ivancovich and to Chuck and Pat Pettis for all their loving support in so many ways.

A landmark in Arizona publishing: "A Gift of Angels: The Art of Mission San Xavier del Bac" by Bernard Fontana with photographs by Edward McCain, 2010.

Late November 2014: San Xavier in early light as seen through the cottonwoods along the Santa Cruz River (Michael McNulty © 2014).